The Big Book of Fenton Milk Glass, 1940-1985

Revised & Expanded 2nd Edition

John Walk

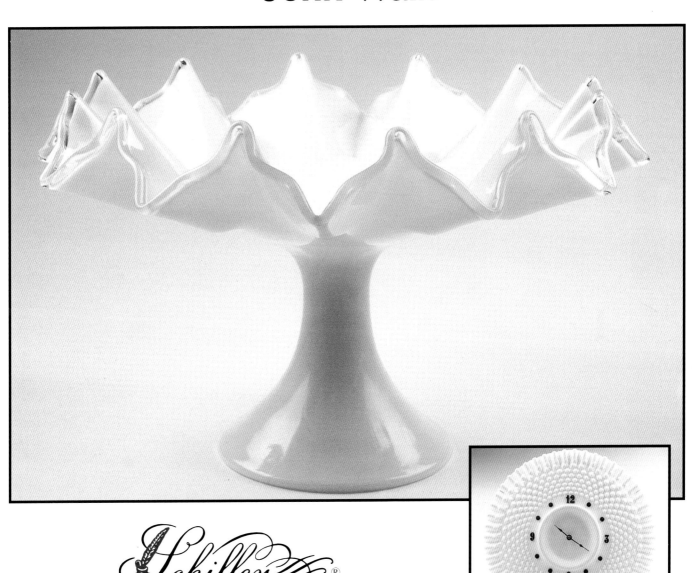

Schiffer Publishing Ltd®

4880 Lower Valley Road, Atglen, PA 19310 USA

Dedication

To Sharen and Al Creery, and Marilyn and Dick Treiweiler, who convinced me of the importance of this Fenton Milk Glass project.

Special Dedication

To Shirley Griffith (May 1935-January 2002): A very special lady who recognized the importance and desirability of Fenton Hobnail Milk Glass. She will be missed by the collectors of Fenton glassware very much.

Revised price guide: 2004
Copyright © 2002 & 2004 by John Walk
Library of Congress Control Number: 2004102529

Designed by "Sue"
Type set in University Roman Bd BT/Souvenir Lt BT

ISBN: 0-7643-2037-8
Printed in China
1 2 3 4

Published by Schiffer Publishing Ltd.
4880 Lower Valley Road
Atglen, PA 19310
Phone: (610) 593-1777; Fax: (610) 593-2002
E-mail: Info@schifferbooks.com
Please visit our web site catalog at
www.schifferbooks.com

This book may be purchased from the publisher.
Include $3.95 for shipping. Please try your bookstore first.
We are always looking for people to write books on new and related subjects. If you have an idea for a book please contact us at the above address.
You may write for a free catalog.

In Europe, Schiffer books are distributed by
Bushwood Books
6 Marksbury Avenue
Kew Gardens
Surrey TW9 4JF England
Phone: 44 (0) 20-8392-8585; Fax: 44 (0) 20-8392-9876
E-mail: info@bushwoodbooks.co.uk
Free postage in the UK. Europe: air mail at cost.

Acknowledgments

First off, thanks to my parents, John W. and Bonnie Walk, who have my undying gratitude. If it were not for them, this book would of not been completed. So many times they have stood up for me over the duration of these Fenton Art Glass book projects. They both were always there when I needed them, to fill in and to do bothersome chores while I was writing this series of books. They cared for me, listened to my fears and thoughts, and wholeheartedly supported me. Thank you from the bottom of my heart.

Over the past two years, my mother, who has always been close to me, accompanied me many times on photo shoots, in spite of her own health problems. She has been a wonderful sounding board when setting pictures. While gathering up glass around different houses, she spots items that I have missed in various collections. During the past year, many times I've wondered what I would do without her! I believe, because of this, we have become closer. I thank her for her sacrifices, help, and support.

Walt Jones of Texas and Darcie Smith of New York have played a large role in helping establish prices for the Hobnail section of this book, watching eBay auctions, consulting with many other collectors, and going with their own gut feelings. I thank them for their time, research, and efforts.

Millie Cody is another person whose help, support, encouragement, and guidance I can never forget. Though I have not known her long, her friendship means more to me than anyone will ever know. She is another individual who, at any time, drops whatever she is doing and comes to my assistance, in proofreading, typing, and many other jobs that make up a book. I can never thank her enough for being there.

Thomas K. Smith, of Indiana, has become a very close friend since I started work on my first book. He is always there to offer ideas, to help with research, and assist in pricing. Over the past few years we have travel together a lot, working both antique and glass shows, and I have come to admire his vast knowledge of all types of glass.

So many other people helped, gave advice, and provided support during the writing of this book. A few of there individuals are Linda Flippen, Thomas K. Smith, Dena & Allen Adden, Don Smith, Lee Garmon, Joyce Lambert, David & Diane Ritter, Roserita Ziegler, Gail Ledbetter, Barbara & Rob Sarver, Bonnie & Frank Zeller, and Alex James & Mike Robbins of James Antiques.

I want to extend a special thanks to Frank Fenton of the Fenton Art Glass Company and Fenton Glass Museum for his help, advice, and support while I have been working on these books over the past few years. He has always been willing to go over the details of my manuscripts, to ferret out mistakes, correct misinformation, or to add in anything the he thinks might be helpful. I know that the average collectors do not realize his love and dedication for the glass that he and his family has produced for almost one hundred years. I also want to thank Jennifer Maston, caretaker of the Fenton Glass Museum, who arranged for me to photograph the glass in the museum collection. She was always ready to help, whenever I needed a question answered or required additional information.

Also, many thanks to Shirley Griffith for her support, encouragement, and help during this project. It is my regret that she did not live to see this volume on the market. It was in the proofing stage at the time of her untimely death in January of 2002. In many ways, the Fenton convention will never be the same for me, or for many others again, because of her absence.

I feel the photographs are the main part of any antiques reference guide. It is true, a picture *is* worth a thousand words. If it were not for the people who opened their homes and collections to me, this book would not have been possible. I am awed and humbled by their generosity. The average person does not realize the efforts that these people make to open up their houses and lives to us so that we can come in to take pictures. Sometimes, because of the amount of glass, we have been there for several days at a time. My thanks goes out to all of you who kept us and welcomed us into your homes. Sharen and Al Creery put up with us for a length of time, and say they are anxious for us to come again. After that long photo session, I don't know whether they love us or are just crazy! Marilyn and Dick Trierweiler actually withstood our onslaught twice! Others who opened up their hearts, lives, and collections to us included:

Williamstown Antique Mall
Linda & John Flippen
Rich & Laurie Karman
Betty & Ike Hardman
Alice & James Rose
Diane & Tom Rohow
Sharen & Al Creery
JR Schonscheck of JR Antiques
Bev & Jon Spencer
Gary & Lynne Virden
Vickie Ticen

Randy Bradshaw
Eileen & Dale Robinson
Marucie Meyes of Mystique Antiques
Randi Jenkins
Melvin & Norma Lampton
Cindy & Rick Blais
Chuck Bingham
Susie, Tiffany, & Ron Ballard
Marilyn & Dick Trierweiler
Wanell & Walt Jones
Darcie Smith
Laurie and Richard Karman
Betty Merrell
Greg & Susan Vail
Harold & Bobbie Morgan
Fran & Bill Ersham

I want to extend my thanks to the Fenton Art Glass Collectors of America and the Fenton Glass Society for the kindness, hospitality, encouragement, and support they have shown me during the past few years at their conventions.

I also want to thank the Fenton Finders Club of Kansas City for their help and hospitality during the Fenton Galas of October 2000 and 2001.

Lastly, I want to thank Peter Schiffer, of Schiffer Publishing, for his support, encouragement, and help throughout this project. Also, many thanks to the staff of Schiffer Publishing, who helped in laying out this volume, and to Jeff Snyder, my editor, for making sense of my ramblings!

FOREWORD TO 2nd EDITION

The response to the first edition of this book has simply amazed me. I knew there were Fenton collectors that loved Milk Glass, but never realized how many—enough to warrant a second edition in a little over a year since the first was published! I had mentioned in the introduction of the first edition that the demand for Milk Glass was increasing and it has continued to do so over the past year, perhaps in part due to it being mentioned on such programs as *Martha Stewart* and others. In seems that in the past year, despite a sluggish economy, Milk Glass is one type of glass in which interest has grown sufficiently.

With this second edition we have updated values and found some items that could not be previously located for the first edition.

As before, if you have questions about this or my other books, or find items that are not listed, please let me know. I can be contacted via email at: jwalk@swetland.net or you can write me at: John Walk, 1962 Memory Lane Rd., Mulberry Grove, IL 62262.

John Walk
2004

Contents

Introduction

Many people asked me *"Why Milk Glass?"* when I started work on this book. Others responded with *"Thank God!"* and *"It's about time, someone did!"* during the same period.

What many people do not realize is that Fenton's Milk Glass, Hobnail Milk Glass, and Silver Crest in general are largely responsible for keeping the Fenton Art Glass Company in business to this day. Fenton Art Glass, during the 1950s, was one of the leading glass companies in the United States in Milk Glass production. At one point, during the 1950s there was close to one hundred items in Hobnail being made in Milk Glass, and over sixty items in Silver Crest, plus other patterns and items that were produced in Milk Glass at the same time.

When my first book, *The Big Book of Fenton,* which was released in 1998, I did not include any Milk Glass, due to of space limitations. At that time, I also did not think it warranted inclusion, based on demand. Boy, was I wrong! I caught it, several times, for not including Milk Glass! Being from the Midwest, there has never been the demand for Milk Glass that there is in the East and West. Now, with the advent of the Internet and eBay, there seems to be more demand for Fenton Milk Glass than there ever was. One fact most people who lent glass for this book have stated is that Milk Glass goes with anything; whatever color you choose to decorate with, Milk Glass works with it.

As the items in different Fenton colors become more scarce and pricey, I see Fenton Milk Glass following the same trend. Demand for Milk Glass is increasing. Many people are incorporating Milk Glass into existing collections of colored Fenton. Established collectors are also scrambling to complete their collections while new collectors are just discovering Milk Glass.

It this book was first conceived, at the outset of this project, as covering only White Milk Glass produced by Fenton. As time wore on, and the deadline approached, many of the items then needed to be pictured in White Milk Glass could not be found, either on the market or in private collections (I *still* don't know where they are hiding!). Because of this, it was decided to include Pastel Milk Glass, which was produced by Fenton from 1954-1958, in order to give the reader a glimpse of many of the shapes that would otherwise only be listed and not pictured. As time passes, I hope to find these other items, so they can be photographed and included in future editions.

The Glass Making Process

A gather of glass is taken from the pot (furnace) of molten glass on the end of a long pipe and is handed to one of the blowers in the shop. On blown ware, a gather of glass is taken from the melting furnace on the end of a long blow pipe and is handed to the blocker or blower. From the blower, who blows the glass into a mould, the piece may be sent either directly to the annealing lehrs for proper cooling or the finisher for further shaping or crimping prior to cooling. Still prior to heading to the lehr, the piece may also be sent to the handler who adds a basket or pitcher handle.

For pressed ware, the gather of glass is dropped into the mould; the presser cuts off the molten glass, and pulls the lever on the press, thereby lowering the plunger into the mould and forcing the glass into all parts of the mould. From there the piece may go to the finisher or handler or directly to the annealing lehrs for cooling.

Chemical List

Opal or Milk Glass	Fluorspar, Feldspar, and Sodium Silicofuroride
Rose Pastel	Selenium, Neodymium, Fluorspar, Feldspar, and Sodium Silicofuroride
Green Pastel	Iron Oxide, Fluorspar, Feldspar, and Sodium Silicofuroride
Blue Pastel	Copper, Chromium, Fluorspar, Feldspar, and Sodium Silicofuroride
Turquoise	Copper, Chromium, Fluorine, and Aluminum

Logos

The now famous "Fenton" in script, in an oval logo, was first used in 1970, only on Carnival Glass. Between 1972 and 1973, it was placed on Hobnail and other items.

By 1975, almost all items made by Fenton had the logo.

In 1980, a small 8 was added to show the decade of the 1980s.

A small F in a logo was used in moulds that were acquired from McKee or moulds purchased from other glass companies. This practice was started in 1983.

The sand blasted logo was used on blown items or limited edition items, where other logos could not be seen. It was also used on off hand items and paste mould items. The sand blasted logo was used from 1980 to 1984.

The fancy script F logo was first sandblasted on Artisan and Connoisseur items beginning in 1984. It is used on items that do not have the regular logo impressed in the mould. Beginning in 1994, this fancy script F replaced the regular logo on all items that had not been previously marked. These items were primarily blown.

In 1990, a small 9 was added to the moulds to show the decade of the 1990s. In some cases, one has to look closely (as the numeral is so small) to determine that it is a 9 and not an 8.

Other markings include the 75th mark above the Fenton logo, used to designate the 75th anniversary items. This practice was continued for each anniversary issue thereafter.

The reader must keep in mind that, even though items made throughout the 1970s and after were to have been marked, there are many, many instances in which the logo was fired out or so faint it is easier to detect by rubbing it with your finger than by seeing it with the naked eye. The type of glass in which the logo was fired out was mostly cased blown ware, such as Cranberry. Sometimes the logo is so faint on these items that all you can make out is part of the oval!

Ware Number Description

In July 1952, Fenton began to assign individual ware numbers to each item. The ware number code included four numerals and two letters. The numbers indicated the pattern and shape while the letters specified the color or decoration. Before July 1952, the mould numbers referred to the pattern or mould shape alone and required a word description following the number to describe shape and color. Example: All Hobnail pieces has the same number, 389. All melon shaped pieces were 192; all sizes and shapes from the same shaped or patterned mould carried the same number.

Color Codes

MI = Milk Glass
BP = Blue Pastel
GP = Green Pastel
RP = Rose Pastel
TU = Turquoise
SC = Silver Crest
CC = Crystal Crest

Pricing

Over the past five years, after observing the Fenton market throughout the United States, I have found that prices are fairly standard in the mainstream market. Of course, prices in some areas are higher then others, while others are much lower.

This book is only intended to be a guide. I can assure you that you will find pieces priced both higher and lower than the values listed here. I am also sure that some readers will not agree with my pricing, but this is a compilation from an intensive price survey, including in the determination of its values both prices realized by dealers selling their glass and prices people have stated that they would be willing to pay for rare items. However, your ultimate guide will always be what you are willing to pay for a piece. Ask yourself how long you can do without that piece in your collection or how much higher you will let the price of an available piece go while you are looking for a more "reasonable" deal.

All prices listed here are retail for mint glassware. Some pieces will be listed as UND (**und**etermined), if the items have proven to be too rare to establish reliable values.

It is not the intention of this author to control or establish prices. As I am also in the business of selling, I know that prices can sometimes be too high and that an overpriced item will not sell.

Measurements

All measurements and terms are from factory catalogs or from actual measurements of the pieces. Actual measurements tend to vary widely from factory catalogs with handmade glass.

History

History of the Fenton Art Glass Company

The Fenton Art Glass Company was organized in July 1905, in Martins Ferry, Ohio, by John, Charles, and Frank L. Fenton. It started as a decorating firm, buying other companies' glass blanks, decorating the items purchased, and then selling the painted glassware. As the Fentons became more competitive with their suppliers, it became necessary that the Fenton Art Glass Company manufacture their own glass.

In January 1907, the Fenton Art Glass Company opened its factory in Williamstown, West Virginia, on the site of the present factory. Their first factory manager was Jacob Rosenthal, creator of Chocolate Glass and Golden Agate. Rosenthal was formerly with the National Glass Company at its plant in Greentown, Indiana, the Indiana Tumbler and Goblet Co., and later with the Evansville Glass Company.

At the onset of manufacturing glass, the Fenton brothers entered the lucrative Carnival and Opalescent Glass market, landing large contracts with Butler Bros. and Woolworth's. Over the next twenty years, the Fenton Glass Company continued to prosper and grow.

In the early 1930s a decline began, which resulted in the most critical period of the company's history. Sales dropped to an all time low in 1933, causing the Fentons to consider closing their doors. Instead, the factory cut expenses, employees wages, and put off improvements in the factory. Money was borrowed from everywhere and insurance polices were mortgaged as orders fell off.

It was during the 1920s Fenton turned away from the now passé Carnival Glass, introducing a line of Stretch Glass and entering into the colored Depression Glass field in the early 1930s. Also added to the Fenton line was a grouping of Opaque colors that became quite popular, including Jade Green, Mongolian Green, Mandarin Red, Periwinkle Blue, Chinese Yellow, Ebony Black, and the now elusive colors of Flame and Lilac. A line of Satin Etch items was introduced in the mid-1930s as the Opaque colors waned in popularity.

It was in 1933 that Fenton introduced its line of mixing bowls and reamers for the Dormeyer company to sell

with its electric egg beaters. It was that account that kept Fenton from folding during the depression years.

A cologne bottle, a copy of the old Hobnail pattern introduced in the late 1930s, pulled the Fenton Art Glass Company from the depths of the Depression and into economic renewal. It was in 1936 that L. G. Wright, a jobber based in New Martinsville, West Virginia (who used Fenton to make glass from moulds that he bought from defunct glass companies), brought in a mould of an old Hobb's Company barber bottle, hoping that Fenton would make a reproduction of it for his wholesale business. Through a chance of fate, a buyer for Wrisley Cologne saw the finished bottle and asked if it could be mass-produced. The original was too expensive to make, but it could be realigned to cut cost; so, the No. 289 bottle was born. The bottles were shipped to Wrisley, who filled and test marketed them in 1938. The result surprised both Fenton and Wrisley as the bottle sold better than they ever hoped, to the point that Fenton could not keep up with the demand. With the Wrisley and Dormeyer accounts, Fenton was quickly operating in the black again.

After seeing the success of the Hobnail cologne bottle, Fenton introduced a complete Hobnail line in 1939, which has become a company mainstay ever since; by far outlasting the Wrisley defection to a machine made bottle in the early 1940s.

Surprisingly, World War II brought a huge increase to Fenton's business in spite of labor and materials shortages. Some lines, such as Topaz Hobnail and Ivory Crest, were completely discontinued because of mineral shortages. Other lines were put on hold at different time until materials were once again available, and other lines were produced without certain chemicals and minerals, changing completely either the color or treatment of that glass (i.e. Blue Opalescent Hobnail became No Opalescent Blue Hobnail and Cranberry Opalescent Hobnail became Ruby Overlay Hobnail).

It was in the 1940s that "Abels Wasserburg" of New York started to buy Fenton products to decorate, as Fenton had done in its early days.

In 1948, the Fenton Company suffered a double loss when Frank L. Fenton passed away in May, followed by his brother Robert in November. This threw Wilmer C.

and Frank M. Fenton, Frank L. Fenton's sons, instantly into the running of the company. Rumors spread quickly during this time that the company was in trouble and planned to fold, causing several major shareholders to sell their stock, which the younger Fenton brothers wisely and quickly bought in the wake of the turmoil.

In the early 1950s it was decided to abandon the independent jobbers, who were essentially in direct competition with the factory authorized stores. Though the cause of some hard feelings with some long time customers, this decision is one of the main reasons for Fenton's survival to this day.

At a time when handmade glass factories were closing rapidly, Fenton chose to expand to compete with the remaining old glass companies and to preserve the sales they had built up during the war. According to an expert in the glass business, the new owners were young and inexperienced and the stockholders lost faith. But, by breaking completely with the past, the Fenton company was able to push ahead. Business procedures were updated, new lines were developed, public relations were promoted, new equipment was bought, and new buildings were built. The product was also improved and strengthen until Fenton was proclaimed as the finest handmade glass in the U.S.

The late 1950s and early 1960s saw rapid rises in sales which surprised even the Fentons! During the mid-1960s, Fenton took advantage of its sales growth to expand its factory and offices. Many new personnel were added to expand the sales force and management of the company. The 1960s were banner years for Fenton.

In the late 1960s, Fenton again turned to hand decorating, with the able hands of Louise Piper and Tony Rosena, who quickly expanded that department into a profitable and long lasting venture. In 1970, Fenton announced the reintroduction of Carnival Glass, which had not been produced by Fenton since the 1920s. To ensure the value of the old pieces, Fenton embossed their name in the new pieces, a practice they would ultimately use on all their glassware. Adding to the strong sales of Carnival Glass in the 1970s was the reintroduction of Burmese, the development of Rosalene, the popular line of Satin Custard colors (along with Milk Glass in Hobnail and Silver Crest), and the still popular Cranberry Opalescent Hobnail.

In the late 1970s, the collector's appeal proved so popular that a collector's club was organized and is now going strong, holding annual conventions in Williamstown, West Virginia, ever summer. The Fenton Museum, dedicated to Fenton Glassware and all glass companies in the mid-Ohio valley, was opened on the second floor of the Fenton factory in 1977.

The 1970s again saw strong sales throughout the decade, in spite of rising cost of materials, union contracts, and expensive energy. In 1978, Frank Fenton decided to relinquish his position as president and became Chairman of the Board. He retired completely in 1985. Bill (Wilmer C.) became President in 1978 and then became Chairman of the Board in 1985 when Frank retired. In 1985, Bill relinquished the presidency to Frank's son, George W., but continued at Chairman of the Board. Frank continues as Vice President of Fenton Gift Shops, Inc. and Historian. Bill is still chairman of the board, President of the Fenton Gift Shop, and is actively involved in promoting the sale of Fenton glass on the QVC Home Shopping Network on cable TV. Their children now run the glass company.

The 1980s were the years of the Fenton company's greatest sales and also their biggest slump in sales. During that decade more glass factories closed and a poor economy developed. In 1979, sales were higher than ever; but, during the next several years a recession developed. Sales fell off and Fenton tried several new ventures in marketing to rebound. One of these, the QVC venture on television, has proven particularly successful. New marketing strategies and private mould work have also helped Fenton rebound from the slump of the 1980s and become stronger than ever.

Throughout the years, the Fenton Art Glass Company has survived tragedies, a devastating Depression, numerous recessions, and labor troubles to become the preeminent handmade glass factory that is not only known nation-wide, but world-wide.

History of the Fenton Milk Glass and Pastel Milk Glass

Several times in the early years of the Fenton Art Glass Company, Milk Glass was produced, but not to a great level. What was listed in Fenton catalogs as a Milk Glass assortment was offered for a short time in the early 1930s. This assortment included the 10" Leaf Tiers Bowl, the Apple Tree Vase, and the Milady Vase, among other things. At around the same time Fenton also produced Moonstone, which was close in appearance to Milk Glass, but with a more opaline effect, that resembled more of a clam broth color.

In 1938, Fenton used large quantities of Milk Glass for the first time when they introduced Peach Blow, which was an Opal (Milk Glass) gather over Ruby. This proved popular and, several years later, the line was revamped by adding a clear edge and was renamed Peach Crest. At the same time, Fenton also introduced Crystal Crest, which was Milk Glass with a clear ring, and an Opal Ring added to the clear ring. Crystal Crest proved costly to make; it was also difficult to get the Opal Ring to stay attached to the clear ring. Crystal Crest was discontinued in less than a year. The product was revamped and produced without the opal ring. This time it was called Silver Crest. This pattern proved very popular and as produced continuously over the next forty years.

Other than Silver Crest, Peach Crest, and the other Colored Crests produced during the 1940s, Fenton did little with Milk Glass. However, in 1950 they introduced their popular Hobnail pattern in Milk Glass, which would become a main stay of their company, for the next thirty-five years. During the same time, Fenton began to produce many smaller lines and accessory items in Milk Glass. Some proved to be popular, lasting several years, and others were swiftly discontinued. This would be the pattern of Milk Glass production over the next thirty years.

It was in 1954, to compete with both Westmoreland and Fostoria, that Fenton introduced a line of colored Milk Glass, which they referred to as Pastel Milk Glass. Those colors were Rose Pastel (Pink), Green Pastel (a light pale Mint Green), and Blue Pastel (a light blue with a lavender cast). In mid-1954, due to the slow sales of the Blue Pastel and Green Pastel, both colors were discontinued and Turquoise (a vibrant Green/Blue color) was introduced. Rose Pastel was discontinued in 1956 and Turquoise was finally discontinued in 1958.

It was also in 1958, to better compete with Westmoreland's and Imperial's pure white Milk Glass, that

Fenton changed its Milk Glass formula. The old formula caused the glass to be more opal in appearance, with lots of fire, whereas the new formula allowed the Milk Glass to be more dense, seeming to be thicker and whiter. In the early 1970s, along with the items produced in color, Fenton adopted their Oval Logo for items produced in Milk Glass.

During the 1970s and early 1980s, Fenton's production of Milk Glass diminished greatly; however, they still presented a good selection of Hobnail and Silver Crest in each of their catalogs. In the mid-1980s Fenton announced that production on Milk Glass Hobnail, and Silver Crest would be halted for a time, due to the public's changing taste and the fact that the fluoride used in making Milk Glass was proving too corrosive to the Day Tanks at the factory, requiring them to be replaced too quickly.

Over next fifteen years, Silver Crest and Hobnail were both produced periodically, in special collections. It is interesting to note that some of these more recent pieces are just as hard to find as the old items!

Patterns in Fenton Milk Glass
1940-1995

Block & Star: MI: 1955-1957; TU: 1955-1956

The Block & Star pattern by Fenton was copied from the an old Hobbs pattern first produced in 1888. Released in 1955 in Turquoise Pastel and Milk Glass, Turquoise was discontinued after a little over a year.

In looking closely at the Block & Star pattern, you can make out a five-point star incised in between the blocks, as if it was trying for an optical illusion within the block pattern.

A total of twenty-eight items were made in this pattern, none of which are regularly seen today. You might keep in mind, while collecting this pattern in Milk Glass, and other Fenton patterns in Milk Glass, that you have serious competition from collectors of Milk Glass in general. Some of these collectors acquire Milk Glass solely because of the color and type of glass, while others are into Victorian and early twentieth century Milk Glass, and pick up Fenton Milk Glass for the quality of the glass.

A rare item to watch out for is the Buffet Set, which consists of two Jam & Jelly Jars and a tray. The Buffet Set tray resembles the regular Jam & Jelly tray, but sits upside down, with indents for the jars to fit into, and has a hole to set it upon a tall glass stand. Keep in mind that this tray rests on a small ledge on the glass stand. It is no wonder that this tray is so hard to find. It was noted at the factory as being difficult to make. Consider the likely survival rate over the years in different homes at busy and rushed breakfasts! Other items to watch for are the 70 oz. jug, the ice tea tumblers, and the little Basket — which never appeared in any Fenton catalogs. This basket looks like the Sugar Bowl with a handle added.

For a full spectrum of Block & Star items, see the color Catalog reprint in the back of *Fenton Glass, The 2nd Twenty-five Years,* by William Heacock, on page 77.

Not Pictured: Milk Glass

Basket, 5637, YOP (**Y**ear(s) **o**f **P**roduction): 7/1955-56, $45-55.
Bowl, Dessert, Square, 5620, YOP: 1955-7/56, $10-15.
Bowl, Dessert, Flared, 5621, YOP: 1955-7/56, $10-15.
Bowl, Dessert, Cupped, 5622, YOP: 1955-7/56, $10-15.
Bowl, Square, 9", 5624, YOP: 1955-7/56, $25-35.
Bowl, Flared, 11", 5625, YOP: 1955-7/56, $25-35.
Candleholder, Square, 5671, YOP: 1955-56, $15-20 each.
Candleholder, Flared, 5672, YOP: 1955-56, $15-20 each.
Candleholder, Cupped, 5673, YOP: 1955-58, $15-20 each.
Jam/Jelly, 5603, YOP: 1955-56, $20-25.
Mayo, 5609, YOP: 1955-56, $25-30.
Relish, 5623, YOP: 1955-7/56, $10-15.
Sugar, 5627, YOP: 1955-7/56, $10-15.
Tumbler, 9 oz., 5649, YOP: 1955-56, $10-15.
Vase, 8.5", 5658, YOP: 1955, $40-50.
Vase, 9", 5659, YOP: 1955, $40-50.

Not Pictured: Turquoise

Basket, 5637, $45-55.
Bonbon, 5635, $15-20.
Dessert, cupped, 5622, $10-15.
Bowl, flared console, 5625, $45-55.
Creamer, 5627, $25-35.
Candlesticks, Cupped, $25-30 each.
Mayonnaise, 5609, $45-55.
Pitcher, 5667, $200-250.
Relish, handled, 5623, $25-65.
Shakers, 5606, $35-45.
Sugar, 5627, $25-35.
Tumbler, 9 oz., 5649, $25-30.
Tumbler, 12 oz., 5647, $30-40.

Candleholder, Handled: 5670, YOP (**Y**ear(s) **o**f **P**roduction): 1955-58, $15-20 each; Bowl, Cupped, 10": 5626, YOP: 1955-56, $25-35. *Courtesy of Diane and Tom Rohow.*

Bowl, Cupped, 10": 5626, $30-40; Candlesticks, Handled: 5760, $25-30 each.

Jam/Jelly on tray, $50-60. *Courtesy of Bobbie & Harold Morgan.*

Buffet Set: 5602, YOP: 1955-7/56, $125-150. *Courtesy of Eileen and Dale Robinson.*

Salt/Pepper: 5606, YOP: 1955-65, $60-70;
Bonbon: 5635, YOP: 1955-58, $10-15.
Courtesy of JR Antiques.

Shakers: 50, $40-50; Jam/Jelly on tray, $90-110.

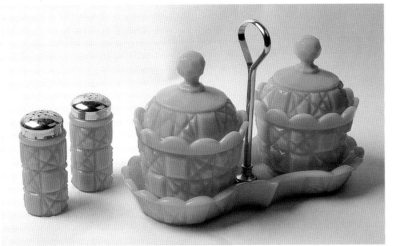

Creamer: 5661, YOP: 1955-7/56, $10-15.

Tumbler, 12 oz.: 5647, YOP: 1955-57,
$15-20; Jug, 70 oz.: 5667, YOP: 1955-57,
$125-150. *Courtesy of Eileen and Dale
Robinson.*

Cactus: 1959-1962; In the Old Virginia Glass Line as Desert Tree: 1967-1970s

Made first in Milk Glass and Topaz Opalescent, Cactus was copied from the old Indiana Tumbler & Glass Co. pattern of the same name. Topaz Opalescent was discontinued after 1960, with Milk Glass being discontinued in 1962. Later in the 1970s and 1980s, the cactus pattern was brought back into several other colors and treatments, including Red Sunset Carnival, Chocolate Glass, and Blue Opalescent. Cactus was reissued in Milk Glass in 1967 by Fenton through their Old Virginia Glass line, which was targeted for sale through both discount and catalog stores.

Scarce items to watch for in Cactus Milk Glass include any baskets, the epergne, cookie jar, cruet, banana bowl, pedestal cake plate, and 6" fan vase.

Not Pictured:

Basket, 10", 3430, YOP: 1959, $45-55.
Bonbon, 3435, YOP: 1959-60, $10-15.
Bowl, 9", 3429, YOP: 1959, $25-430.
Banana Bowl, 3425, YOP: 1959, $35-40.
Candy Jar, 3480, YOP: 1959-60, $65-75.
Candy Box, 3488, YOP: 1959-62, $35-45.
Goblet, 3445, YOP: 1959-62, $10-15.
Sugar, 3404, YOP: 1959, $20-30.
Vase, 5", 3454, YOP: 1959-7/59, $10-15.
Vase, Fan, 6", 3459, YOP: 1959, $30-35.
Vase, 7", 3456, YOP: 1959-60, $20-25.
Vase, Footed, 3460, 7/59-62, $20-30.
Vase, Medium, 3461, 7/59-60, $25-35.
Vase, Tall, 3452, YOP: 7/59-12/59, $35-40.

Bowl, 8": 3429, YOP: 1959-7/59, $25-30; Bowl, 8", Ftd.: 3422, YOP: 1959-60, $40-50. *Courtesy of Cindy and Rick Blais.*

Basket, 7": 3437, YOP: 1959, $35-40.

Basket, 9": 3439, YOP: 1959, $35-40; Bonbon. 3435, YOP: 1959-60, $10-15; Vase, 7": 3456, YOP: 1959-60, $20-25.

Epergne: 3401, YOP: 1959, $75-100. *Courtesy of Mildred & Roland Potter.*

Cruet: 3463, YOP: 1959-60, $45-55.

Nut Dish, Footed: 3428, YOP: 1959-62, $15-20. *Courtesy of Mystique Antiques.*

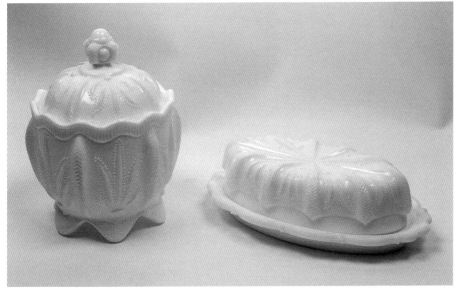

Covered Sugar: 3408, YOP: 1959, $25-30; Butter, 1/4 lb.: 3477, YOP: 1959-60, $25-35. *Courtesy of Williamstown Mall.*

Candleholders: 3474, YOP: 1959-7/60, $15-20. each

Salt/Pepper: 3406, YOP: 1959-62, $15-20.

15

Plate, Footed, 11": 3412, YOP: 1959, $30-40.
Courtesy of Cindy and Rick Blais.

Plate, 11": 3411, YOP: 1959, $15-20. (Shown upside down, so the pattern shows. The top is plain displaying no pattern. See Footed Plate, previous picture.) *Courtesy of Randi Jenkins.*

Creamer: 3404, YOP: 1959, $20-30; Sugar: 3408, YOP: 1959, $25-30; Epergne: 3401, YOP: 1959, $75-100; Vase, 9": 3459, YOP: 7/59-60, $25-30. *Courtesy of Bobbie & Harold Morgan.*

Vase, 7": 3457, YOP: 1959-7/59, $20-25;
Vase, bud, 8": 3450, YOP: 7/59-64, $10-15.

Daisy & Button: MG: 1953-1962 (In the Old Virginia Glass Line 1969-mid-1970s); GP/BP: 1/1954-7/1954; RP: 1954-1956; Turquoise: 1955-1956

Daisy & Button was first introduced in the late 1930s by Fenton. Due to a lack of accurate catalogs from that period, it is difficult to pinpoint what colors and items were produced during the 1930s. Also, the fact that L. G. Wright had a Daisy & Button line at the same time makes it somewhat more difficult to determine what was made by Fenton and what was produced by L. G. Wright. Many of the same colors were in use by Fenton and L. G. Wright at the same time! We do know that colors made by Fenton in the 1930s in Daisy & Button included Crystal, Cape Cod Green, Wisteria, Topaz, and both French and Blue Opalescent. We also know that three different sizes of top hats, along with the cat slipper, the hand cornucopia vase, and the fan tray were also made at that time. Perhaps the most desirable colored item in Daisy & Button, the 10" Fan Vase, was also made in the 1930s. It is somewhat ironic that this item, which was classified as the Cape Cod design and not Daisy & Button, would later become a Daisy & Button item. Keep in mind that, when Daisy & Button and Cape Cod were first issued, Daisy & Button was an over all design, while Cape Cod had plain panels on it. In the 1950s, when Fenton issued Daisy & Button in Milk Glass, they used more Cape Cod moulds for that pattern than actual Daisy & Button moulds.

In 1953, Fenton issued Daisy & Button in Milk Glass, in approximately twenty-five items. It became a good selling and popular pattern, lasting until 1962. Beginning in 1954, Daisy & Button was produced in all colors of Pastel Milk Glass. It was reissued in Milk Glass, though Old Virginia Glass, for several years beginning in 1969. In this section, we are placing all Daisy & Button items, whether they were made by Fenton, for Fenton, or by Fenton for Old Virginia Glass. For more information on Old Virginia Glass, see the finial chapter in this book.

Scare items to find in Daisy & Button, in Milk Glass, include any size of basket and the two light candleholder.

Not Pictured: Daisy & Button

Basket, 4", 1934, YOP: 1953-55, $25-35.
Basket, 5", 1935, YOP: 1953-55, OVG: 1970s, $35-45.
Basket, 10.5", 1930, YOP: OVG: 1970s, $40-45.
Bowl, Square, 10.5", 1920, YOP: 1953-62, $25-35.
Bowl, Oval, 1921, YOP: OVG: 1970s, $25-35.
Bowl, Footed, 1922, YOP: 1954-59, $35-45.
Bowl, Footed, 1924, YOP: 1954-60, $40-50.
Bowl, Footed, 1926, YOP: 1954-6/56, $35-45.
Candleholder, 1970, YOP: OVG: 1970s, $15-20 each.
Candleholder, 2 Light, 1974, YOP: 1953-62, $25-30 each.
Hat #1, 1991, YOP: 1953-56, $15-20.
Hat #2, 1992, YOP: 1953-56, OVG: 1970s, $15-20.
Hat #3, 1993, YOP: 1953-6/56, $10-15.
Vase, 3", 1953, YOP: 1953-55, $10-15.
Vase, Footed, 8", 1957, YOP: 1953-58, $30-40.
Vase, Footed, 8", 1958, YOP: 1953-60, OVG: 1970s, $35-40.

Basket, Oval, split handle: 1939 (**O**ld **V**irginia **G**lass (OVG) 1970s), $20-25.

Bowl, Cupped, 7": 1927, YOP: 1953-58, $20-30.

Bowl, Oval, 9": 1929, YOP: 1953-6/59, OVG: 1970s, $25-35.

Bowl, 7", cupped: 1927, $35-45; Vase, footed fan, 8": 1959, $45-55; Bowl, 9" oval: 1929, $45-60; Boot: 1994, $45-55; Vase, footed, 8": 1957, $40-50.

Slipper: 1995, YOP: 1953-6/56, 1985, OVG: 1970's, $10-15; Boot: 1990, YOP: OVG 1970s, $10-15; Boot, YOP: 1953, $15-20. *Courtesy of Bobbie & Harold Morgan.*

Sugar/Creamer: 1903, YOP: 1953-6/56, OVG: 1970s, $15-20 ea; Basket, 6": 1936, YOP: 1953-58, $20-30; Bon bon: 1937, YOP: 1953-6/56, $10-15; Vase, 4": 1954, YOP: 1953-64, $10-15. *Courtesy of Bobbie & Harold Morgan.*

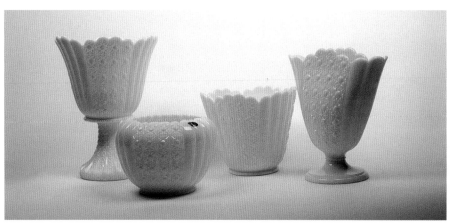

Vase, Ftd.: 1955, YOP: 1954-59, $25-35; Bowl, Cupped, 7": 1927, YOP: 1953-58, $20-30; Vase, 6": 1956, YOP: 1953-56, $25-35. *Courtesy of Bobbie & Harold Morgan.*

Sugar/Creamer: 1903, YOP: 1953-6/56, OVG: 1970, $15-20 each.

Salt/Pepper: 1906, (OVG: 1970s), $15-20. *Courtesy of Melvin and Norma Lampton.*

Candy, Covered: 1980 (OVG: 1970s), $30-35.   Boots: 1994, $45-55.

Boot: 1953, $15-20.

Fan Vase, 9", footed: 1959, YOP: 1953-7/62, OVG: 1970, $40-45.

Diamond Lace: MG: 1952-1964,
TU: 1955-1956

Introduced in 1948 in Blue and French Opalescent, the Diamond Lace pattern was included among many other Fenton patterns slated, in 1952, for inclusion in their full scale production of Milk Glass. One item in Diamond Lace was issued in Turquoise in 1956; that was the #4808 3 horn Epergne.

Not Pictured: Diamond Lace

Epergne, 4802, TU, YOP: 1955-56, $150-200.

Epergne, 1 Horn: 4801, YOP: 6/1952-56, $75-85; Candlesticks, Cornucopia: 1948, YOP: 1952-53, $20-25 each; Epergne, 3 Horn: 4802, YOP: 1956-64, $45-55. *Courtesy of Tom and Diane Rohow.*

Figurals

Although Fenton did not release as many of their figurals in Milk Glass as they did in other colors, some Milk Glass examples were incorporated into their regular lines. Also keep in mind that any figurals that were used in decorated patterns in Milk Glass from the 1970s and 1980s could have escaped from the decorators and been sold in the Fenton Gift Shop in plain Milk Glass.

Not Pictured: Figurals

Butterfly, 5170, YOP: 1970, $15-20.
Chick Server, 5189, YOP: 1954-6/56, $200-250.

Madonna Vase: 5157, YOP: 1953-56, $25-35. *Courtesy of Melvin and Norma Lampton.*

Owl Decision Maker: 5157, YOP: 1969-72, $25-30. *Courtesy of Melvin and Norma Lampton.*

Cat: 5165, $35-40; Butterfly on Stand: 5171, $30-40.

Cat: 5165, $35-40; Kitten: 5119, $30-35. *Courtesy of Myers Mystique.*

Elephant: 5108, $500+.

Apple: 5019, $35-45. *Courtesy of Susie, Tiffany, and Ron Ballard.*

Alley Cat: 5177, $85-95.

Hobby Horse: 5135, $30-35.

Hen on Nest:, YOP: 1953-56, $30-35. (Note the difference in bases, hence the reason for the different ware numbers.) *Courtesy of Melvin and Norma Lampton.*

Santa Light: 5106, YOP: 1970-77, $45-55.

Hen On Nest, Small: 5186, YOP: 1967-72, $25-30.

Santa In Chimney Music Box: 5235, $75-85. *Courtesy* of Chuck Bingham

Hen On Nest, Large: 5182, YOP: 1967-72, $40-45; Bird (Happiness): 5197, YOP: 1953-55, $20-25; Turtle Ring Tree: 9199, YOP: 1969-72, $10-15.

Chick on Nest: 5185, YOP: 1953-7/56, $65-75. *Courtesy of Alice and James Rose.*

Flower Panel: MI: 1958-1959

This pattern was applied to a unique condiment set. The set was produced with the shakers and mustard made in both Milk Glass and Jamestown Blue Transparent. Sets were sold both ways on a triangular Lace Edge plate. This set is both rare and desirable.

Not Pictured: Flower Panel

Salt/Pepper, 6206, 1958, $15-20.

Tri Plate, Lace Edge: 6219, YOP: 1958-59, $15-20; Mustard: 6289, YOP: 1958-59, $10-15.

Hobnail: MI: 1950-1990s

I do not think the Fenton Glass Company realized, when the Hobnail pattern in Milk Glass was first issued, that it would become a mainstay of their factory for over thirty years. It is the longest running color, aside from Cranberry Opalescent in Hobnail, that Fenton produced in the Hobnail pattern. The Hobnail pattern in Milk Glass was also produced in more pieces than any other pattern made by Fenton.

Throughout the years, Milk Glass Hobnail has developed almost what could be a called a cult following. I suspect, from working with different collectors while writing this book, that the Milk Glass collectors who collect both Hobnail and Silver Crest are more devout and fanatical than the collectors of any other type of Fenton Art Glass!

In the mid-1980s, when Fenton announced that it would stop full time production of Milk Glass in Hobnail due to the cost factor involved, the outcry was overwhelming. Since then, it has been reissued several times throughout the 1990s in limited issues.

Keep in mind that, due to the changing of the Milk Glass formula in 1958, many pieces will look different in color and will have more fire when held up to the light.

Also keep in mind that Fenton produced a short issue of Hobnail in Milk Glass in the 1940s. This issue consisted largely of two sizes of Goblets, a Sherbet, 8" Plate, and three sizes of Tumblers. I can tell no difference between these items and the ones made off the same moulds in the 1950s.

Due to the many items produced in Hobnail Milk Glass, the list of scare items is huge. The rare items include the clover leaf relish (without the dividers in the center), the 16 oz. Flat Tumblers, the 3 oz. Wine Goblet, and the Footed 3-horn Epergne. The epergne had a limited run of about one year and was made up of the #3920 Comport, 3-horns from the mini epergne, and a small round three hole flower block (Flower Frog) that rested in the comport and held the horns. Most of these are now either lying around some home, with the owners not having any idea of what they were used for, or they are resting in a collection of Flower Frogs, with their true intent and identity hidden from their owners!

Not Pictured: Hobnail

Relish, Undivided, 3822, 1954, $600+.
Wine Goblet, 4 oz., 3853, $125-150.
Lamp, Pillar, 3907, $300+.
Vase, 3755, $300+

Cigarette Lighter: 3692, $20-25, YOP: 6/1962-74; Cigarette Box: 3685, YOP: 1961-71, $35-40; Ash Tray, Ball: 3648, YOP: 1977-78, $45-55; Ashtray, Square, 5": 3679, YOP: 1961-77, $20-25.

Below:
Ashtray, #3: 3878, YOP: 6/1945-64, $25-30; Ashtray, #2: 3877, YOP: 6/1954-67/68, $20-25; Ashtray, #1: 3876, YOP: 6/1954-66, $15-20; Ashtray, Pipe: 3693, YOP: 6/1962-75, $10-15; Ashtray, Small: 3972, YOP: 1964-67/68, $10-15; Ashtray, Medium: 3973, YOP: 1966-7/68, $15-20; Ash Tray, Round: 3776, YOP: 1964-67, $20-25.

Ashtray, Pipe: 3773, YOP: 1963-67/68, $70-80; Ashtray/Chip 'n' Dip/Candle Bowl: 3778, YOP: 1971-89, $30-35.

Basket, 7" Deep: 3637, $100-125 (Notice difference in Crimp-NIL). *Courtesy of Cindy & Rick Blais.*

Basket, 5.5": 3735, YOP: 1971-84, $25-35; Basket, 5.5": 3835, YOP: ???, $45-55; Basket, 6.5": 3736, YOP: 1958-84, $40-45.

Basket, Looped Handle: 3335, YOP: 6/92-6/92, $40-45.

Basket, 7": 3837, YOP: 1952-89, $35-40.

Basket, 4.5": 3336, YOP: 1992-94, $25-30; Basket, 10":
3830, YOP: 6/1953-89, $55-65; Basket, 4.5": 3834, YOP:
1952-89, $25-30.

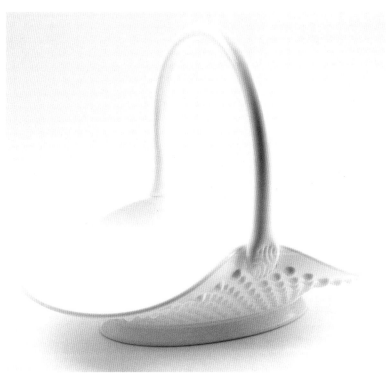

Basket, Oval, 12": 3839, YOP: 1983, $150+. *Courtesy of
Walt and Wanell Jones.*

Basket, Oval: 3634, YOP: 1963-67/68, $45-50; Basket, Oval, 12":
3839, YOP: 1960-74, $80-90; Basket, Oval, 6.5": 3838, YOP:
1961-67/68, $40-50.

Basket, 8.5": 3638, YOP: 1968/69-89, $45-55.

Basket, 12": 3734, YOP: 6/1959-89, $60-65; Basket, Deep, 7": 3637, YOP: 1963-77, $80-90.

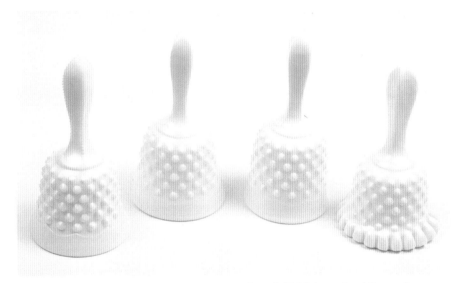

Bells: 3667 (all except the one on the right), YOP: 1967-86 (note the different Crimps, Flares and handles on these; left is pre logo and has small beads along edges of handle). $15-25; Bell: 3645, YOP: 1991-95, $35-40.

Nut Dish, Oval: 3732, YOP: 1958-65, $20-25; Nut Dish, Round, Handled: 3729, YOP: 1957-64, $40-45; Nut Dish, Footed: 3631, YOP: 1962-67/68, $35-40; Nut Dish, Oval: 3633, YOP: 1968/69-89, $15-20.

Back: Bonbon, 2 Handled, 7.25": 3937, YOP: 1952-76, $15-20; Bonbon, Star: 3921, YOP: 1953-69, $15-20; Bonbon, Handled, 5": 3935, YOP: 1952-6/56, $20-25. Front: Bonbon: 3630, YOP: 1961-77, $10-15; Bonbon, 6": 3926, YOP: 1952-89, $10-15.

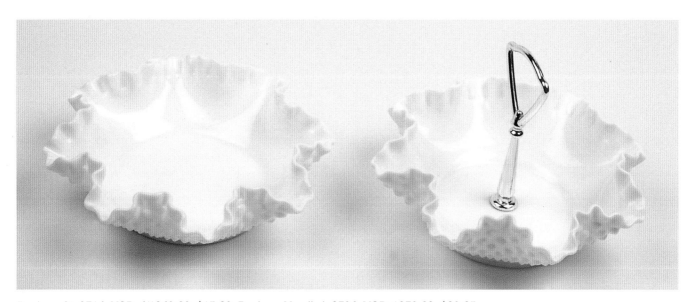

Bonbon, 8": 3716, YOP: 6/1960-80, $15-20; Bonbon, Handled: 3706, YOP: 1970-89, $20-25.

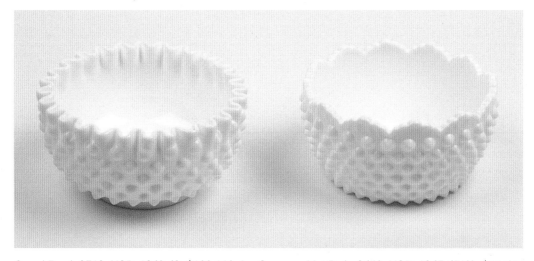

Cereal Bowl: 3719, YOP: 1960-63, $100-110; Ice Cream or Nut Dish: 3650, YOP: 1967-67/68, $55-65.

Bowl, Rose, "Wavy Hobnail": 3022, YOP: 1987-88, $40-50.

Chip 'N Dip: 3703, YOP: 1958-79, $55-60.

Chip 'N Dip: 3922, YOP: 1970, $750+. *Courtesy of Wanell and Walt Jones.*

Bowl, 12": 3938, YOP: 1960-89, $40-45; Bowl, 7": 3927, YOP: 1952-80, $10-15; Bowl, 9": 3924, YOP: 1952-88, $20-25.

Bowl, Large Square: 3929, YOP: 1954-6/61, $100-125; Bowl, Square
Berry: 3928, YOP: 1954-67/68, $15-20.

Bowl, 8.5", 3-Footed: 3724, YOP: 1958-77, $45-50.

Bowl, D.C., 10": 3624, YOP: 1961-84, $35-45.

Bowl, 8": 3639, YOP: 1970-78, $30-35; Bowl, Oval, 8": 3625, YOP: 1961-78, $25-35;
Bowl, 3-Toed: 3635, 1963-89, $15-20.

Bowl, 8": 3626, YOP: 1961-67/68, $35-45; Candleholder, Footed: 3673, YOP: 1963-75, $15-20 each.

Bowl, Cupped: 3735, YOP: 6/1959-64, $175-200; Candleholder: 3770, YOP: 6/1959-64, $65-75 each.

Bowl, 10.5": 3623, YOP: 1961-64, $200-225. *Courtesy of Sharen and Al Creery.*

Bowl, Shallow, 9.5": 3622, YOP: 1961-78, $55-65. *Courtesy of Sharen and Al Creery.*

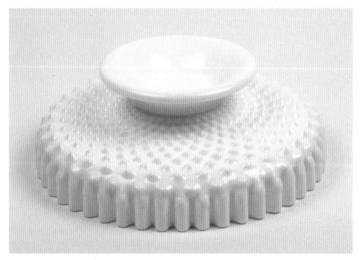

Shallow Bowl, Reverse Side.

Bowl, Oval, Footed, 9": 3621, YOP: 1970-76, $45-55.

Bowl, Footed: 3723, YOP: 1957-77, $50-60; Comport, 10": 3731, YOP: 6/1959-79, $35-40.

Bowl, Footed: 3723, YOP: 1957-77, $75-80. Notice the difference in the crimp! *Courtesy of Sharen and Al Creery.*

Below:
Banana Bowl, Low: 3620, YOP: 1961-78, $45-55; Banana Bowl: 3720, YOP: 6/1959-83, $50-60.

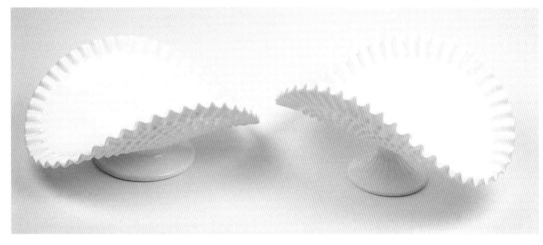

Below:
Punch Set, 14 piece: 3908, $600-625. This set consists of the Octagon 3820 Punch Bowl, YOP: 6/1953-57, $250-265; Octagon Punch Cup: 3840, YOP: 1953-58, $30-35; and the Punch Ladle: 9520, YOP: 7/53-59, $65-75. *Courtesy of Sharen and Al Creery.*

Punch Set, 15 piece: 3807, $572-600. This set consists of the 3847 Punch Cup, YOP: 1952-65, $20-25; 3817, 16" Torte Plate, YOP: 1952-6/59, $150-175; the Punch Ladle: 9520, YOP: 7/53-59, $65-75; and the 3827 Punch Bowl: YOP: 1952-58, $125-150.

Punch Bowl Set with Handle: 389, $500+. *Courtesy of Wanell and Walt Jones.*

Punch Set with Crimp and Cupped Bowl: $500+.

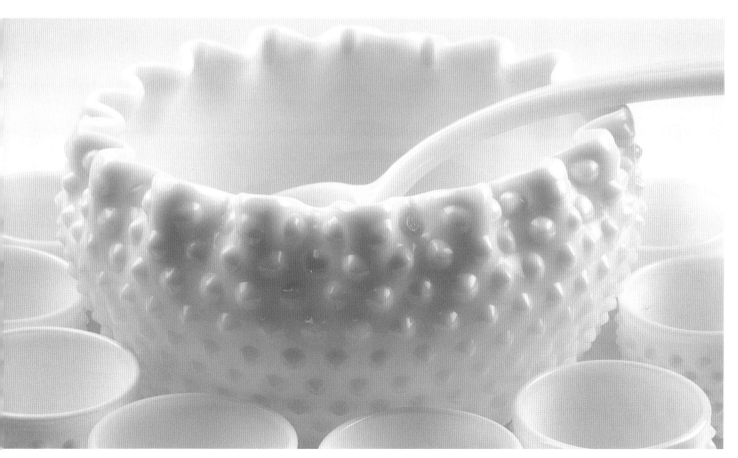

View of the ruffle of the Crimped and Cupped Punch Bowl.

Punch Set, 15 piece: 3712, YOP: 1958-66, $525-550. This set consists of the 3778 Punch Bowl Base, $100-125; 3722, 7 Qt. Punch Bowl, $125-150; and the 3847 Punch Cup, $20-25. *Courtesy of Sharen and Al Creery.*

Vanity Bottle: 3986, YOP: 1953-54, $690+. *Courtesy of Wanell and Walt Jones.*

Back: Vanity Bottle: 3986, YOP: 1953-54, $650+; Cologne Bottles: 3865, YOP: 1955-6/56, $40-50; Puff Box: 3885, YOP: 1955-6/56, $75-85. Front: Vanity Tray: 3775, YOP: 1960-64, $150-175. *Courtesy of Sharen and Al Creery.*

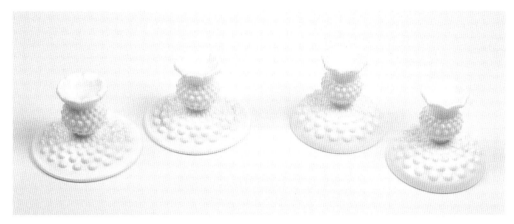

Candleholders, Flat and Rounded: 3974, YOP: Flat: 1952-54, $40-45; Rounded: 1955-79, $35-40.

Candleholders, Handled: 3870, YOP: 1953-73, $35-40 each; Candleholders Cornucopia: 3874, YOP: 6/1953-64, $35-40 each; Cornucopias, Mini: 3971, YOP: 1952-6/56, $30-35 each.

Candleholders, 6": 3674, YOP: 1961-89, $20-25 each; Candleholders, 2 Light: 3672, YOP: 1961-70, $55-65 each; Candleholders, 10": 3774, YOP: 1958-66, $35-40 each.

Footed Candleholders, made from the 3728 Comport, $75-85 each.

Candle Bowl: 3771, YOP: 6/1959-67/68, $30-35; Candleholders: 3775, YOP: 1972-76, $25-30 each.

Crescent Holder: 3678, YOP: 1962, $500+. *Courtesy of Sharen and Al Creery.*

Candleholder, 7": 3745, YOP: 1961-89, $40-45 each; Petite Epergne: 3671, YOP: 1961, $35-40 (Sold together as the 3902 Petite Epergne Set); Candelabra or Centerpiece, 3 piece: 3742, $175-200 each (consisting of the 3774 10" Candleholder, $35-40 each; 3746 Candle Epergne, $50-55; and 3748 Chip 'N Dip/Candle Bowl, YOP: 1973-75, $60-65); Candleholder, 10": 3774, YOP: 1958-66, $35-40 each; Candle Epergne: 3746, YOP: 1973-75, $50-55.

Candle Bowl: 3872, YOP: 1970-87, $15-25;
Candle Bowl, Mini: 3873, YOP: 1968/69-76,
$25-30 each; Candle Bowl, Footed: 3971,
YOP: 1978-79, $60-65.

Butter, Covered Oval: 3777, YOP:
1970-89, $30-35; Butter/Cheese,
Covered: 3677, YOP: 1961-67/68,
$150-200; Butter, Covered: 3977,
YOP: 6/1954-77, $25-30.

Oil/Mustard, on Tray: 3715, YOP:
1956-61, $60-65; Sugar/Creamer
Set, On Tray: 3917, YOP: 1955-83,
$35-40.

Oil/Vinegar, on Tray: 3916, YOP: 1955-77,
$50-55; Jam/Jelly, on Tray: 3915, YOP: 1955-
74, $70-75.

Condiment Set: 3809 (consisting of the 3879 Handled Tray, 3900 Sugar/Creamer, 3869 Oil, 3889 Mustard, and 3806 Salt/Pepper), YOP: 1952-73, $150-175.

Back: Oil, 7 oz.: 3767, YOP: 1956-64, $50-55; Cruet: 3863, YOP: 1952-74, $50-55; Oil: 3869, YOP: 1952-72, $15-20. Front: Jam Set: 3903, YOP: 1952-73, $35-40; Mustard: 3889, YOP: 1952-67/ 68, $25-30; Mayonnaise Set: 3803, YOP: 1952-83, $30-35.

Back: Creamer/Sugar: 3708, YOP: 1956-67/68, Creamer: $15-20, Sugar: $15-20; Creamer/Sugar: 3901, YOP: 1952-67/68, Creamer: $12-15, Sugar: $12-15; Creamer/Sugar: 3906, YOP: 1952-80, Creamer: $10-15, Sugar: $10-15. Front: Creamer/Sugar: 3900, YOP: 1952-72, Creamer: $5-10, Sugar: $5-10; Creamer, Mini: 3665, YOP: 1965-1967/68, $15-20; Creamer/Sugar: 3702, YOP: 1970-73, Creamer: $20-25, Sugar: $20-25.

Creamer/Sugar, Covered: 3606, YOP: 1961-89,
Creamer: $15-20, Sugar: $20-25; Jam Jar,
Covered: 3601, YOP: 1970-81, $50-55;
Creamer/Sugar, Covered: 3902, YOP: 1970-83,
Creamer: $15-20, Sugar: $20-25; Mustard,
Covered: 3605, YOP: 1970-76, $30-35.

Cinnamon Shaker: 3797, $150-175; Salt/Pepper: 3609, YOP:
1966-89, $25-30; Kitchen Salt/Pepper: 3602, YOP: 1962-78, $25-
30; Salt/Pepper: 3806, YOP: 1952-84, $20-25. (The Black Shakers
were sold with the Milk Glass Shakers in a special promotion in
1968 in the Fenton Gift Shop at the same time that Ebony Crest
was sold at the Gift Shop. Values for the Black Shakers are the
same as the Milk Glass.)

Pickle Dish, 8" Oval: 3640,
YOP: 1964-83, $15-20.

Celery, 12": 3739, YOP: 6/1959-62, $350-375; Relish,
Divided, 12": 3740, YOP: 6/1959-82, $50-55.

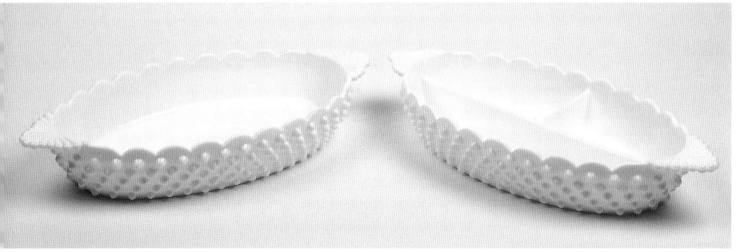

Relish, Handled: 3607, YOP: 1970-84, $35-40.

Relish, Heart Shaped: 3733, YOP: 1958-86, $35-40; Margarine Tub: 3802, YOP: 1974-89, $30-35; Relish, Heart Shaped, without Handle: 3033, YOP: 1987-89, $45-55.

Salad Dressing Set, on Wooden Tray, using two 3928 small square bowls, with wooden lids, and a wooden tray. Jam set using two 3990 Kettles with wooden lids on a wooden tray, assembled by Kennedy Bros. Bristol, Vermont, YOP: Mid-1960s. Salad Dressing Set: UND; Jam Set: UND.

Back side of Wooden Tray, showing the Kennedy Bros Stamp.

Variety of Fenton Hobnail Milk Glass items that Kennedy Bros. used to create sets. *Courtesy of Sharen and Al Creery.*

Condiment Set, Kennedy Bros.: made up of the Wooden Tray, Wooden Shakers, two 3990 Mustard Kettles with Wooden Lids, and two 3869 Oil Bottles (original Oil Bottles had wooden stoppers.), UND. *Courtesy of Wanell and Walt Jones.*

Condiment Sets, Kennedy Bros.: Left: Set made up with a Wooden Lazy Susan; three 3990 Mustard Kettles with Wooden Lids; Right: Set made up with a Wooden Lazy Susan, two 3896 Oil Bottles with Wooden Stoppers, and two 3605 Mustards with Wooden Lids, UND. *Courtesy of Melvin and Norma Lampton.*

Comport, Footed: 3628, YOP: 1962-89, $15-20; Comport, Footed: 3728, YOP: 1956-82, $15-20; Nut Dish, Footed: 3629, YOP: 1962-89, $20-25; Jelly Dish, Footed: 3725, YOP: 1958-67/68, $30-35; Peanut Dish, Footed: 3627, YOP: 1962-77, $15-20; Nut Dish, Footed: 3629, YOP: 1962-89, $15-20

Comport, Footed: 3920, YOP: 1959-79, $20-25; Comport, Low Footed: 3727, YOP: 1958-79, $15-25.

Candy Jar, Flat: 3880, YOP: 1952-75, $35-40; Candy Jar, Footed: 3980, YOP: 1952-75, $40-45.

Candy Box: 3984, YOP: 1974-77, $175-200; Candy, Butterfly Cover: 3600, YOP: 1971-89, $35-45; Candy Box: 3668, YOP: 1975-89, $55-65; Candy Jar: 3688, YOP: 1963-76, $45-50.

Honey Jar: 3886, YOP: 1953-59, $100-125; Candy Box, Footed: 3784, YOP: 1968/69-81, $40-45; Candy Jar, Footed: 3886, YOP: 1968/69-89, $45-50; Candy Dish, Oval: 3786, YOP: 1960-81, $30-35.

Candy Box, Footed: 3885, YOP: 1968/69-77, $45-50; Comport, Covered Footed: 3887, YOP: 6/1953-67/68, $40-45.

Candy Jar: 3883. YOP: 1953-67/68. $40-45.

Cookie Jar: 3680. YOP: 1962-73. Pre-Logo, $125-150; with Logo, $65-70.

Candy Bowl, Ribbon Crimp: 3730. YOP: 6/1959-61. $225-250.

Apothecary Jar: 3689, YOP: 1964-72, $200-225;
Wedding Jar: 3780, YOP: 1957-76, $40-45; Urn,
Covered: 3986, YOP: 1968-69, $550+. *Courtesy
of Sharen and Al Creery.*

Epergne, 5 piece: 3800, YOP: 1954, $600+.
Courtesy of Wanell and Walt Jones.

Breakdown of #3800 Epergne.

Urn, Covered: 3986, YOP: 1968-69, $550+.
Courtesy of Sharen and Al Creery.

Epergne, 4 piece: 3701, YOP: 7/
1956-83, $60-65; Epergne, 2
piece: 3704, YOP: 1975-77,
$100-110; Epergne, Mini, 4
piece: 3801, YOP: 1952-77,
$75-85.

Decanter: 3761, YOP: 1960-67/68, $225-250; Goblet,
Wine: 3843, YOP: 6/1960-67/68, $30-35.

Jug, Tankard: 389, $500+. *Courtesy of Betty and
Ike Hardman.*

Tumbler, 12 oz.: 3947,
YOP: 6/1953-53, $350+.

Back: Jug, Squat: 3965, YOP: 1952-67/68, $50-55; Jug, 80 oz.: 3967, YOP: 6/1953-67/68, $125-150; Jug, Ice Lipped, 70 oz.: 3664, YOP: 1964-5/73, 1974-89, $60-70; Jug, 54 oz.: 3764, YOP: 1958-80, $65-75. Front: Pitcher, 12 oz.: 3762, YOP: 1958-78, $35-45.

Jug, 80 oz.: 3967, YOP: 6/1953-67/68, $125-150; Tumbler, 16 oz.: 3946, YOP: 6/1956-56, $500+. *Courtesy of Wanell and Walt Jones.*

Pitcher: 3360, $75-85; Bowl: 3938, $40-45. Sold as a set, 3000, YOP: 1992-94.

Sherbet: 3825, YOP: 1954-67/68, $15-25; Goblet: 3845, YOP: 1954-74, $15-20.

Fairy Light, 3 piece: 3804, YOP: 1975-81, $150-165; Fairy Light: 3608, YOP: 1968/69-82, $25-35.

Tumbler, 5 oz.: 3945, YOP: 1952-67/68, $10-15; Tumbler, 12 oz.: 3942, YOP: 1954-67/68, $15-20; Tumbler, 9 oz.: 3949, YOP: 6/1953-92, $15-20; Ice Tea, Footed: 3842, YOP: 1954-67/68, $25-35.

Lamp, Mini: 3305, YOP: 1/87-6/87, $90-100.
Courtesy of Sharen and Al Creery.

Lamp, Courting, Electric: 3793, YOP: 1965-71, $150-200; Lamp, Courting, Oil: 3792, YOP: 1965-71, $200-225.

Hurricane Lamp, 11": 3713, YOP: 1979-80, $300-400; Hurricane Lamp: 3998, YOP: 1952-69, $70-80. *Courtesy of Sharen and Al Creery.*

Lamp, Student, 21": 3807, YOP: 1971-89/91-92, $225-250; Lamp, Prism, 22.5": 1174, YOP: 1993-95, $350-375. *Courtesy of Sharen and Al Creery.*

Lamp, Student, 18.5" with Ball Shade: YOP: 1993, $175-200; Lamp, Student, 19": 3707, YOP: 1966-76, $275-300.

Lamp, GWTW, 22": 3808, YOP: 1976-95, $225-250.

Stein, 14 oz.: 3646, YOP: 1977-79, $150-175. *Courtesy of Sharen and Al Creery.*

Egg Cup: 3647, YOP: 1970-71, $90-100.

Childs Cup: 489, YOP: 1950-51, $120-130; Pitcher, 7": 3365, YOP: 1992-94, $65-75; Spoon Holder: 3612, YOP: 1967-68, $90-100; Salt Dips: 9496, sold originally as a set of four, YOP: 1988, $225-250 for the set of four. *Courtesy of Sharen and Al Creery.*

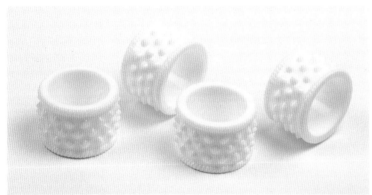

Napkin Rings: 3904, sold originally as a set of four, YOP: 1976-77, $175-200.

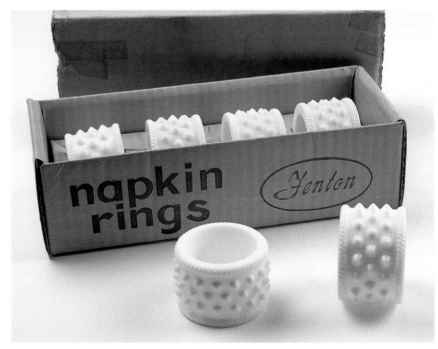

Napkin Rings: 3904, shown in original box, YOP: 1976-77, $225-250. *Courtesy of Wanell and Walt Jones.*

Hanging Bowl: 3705, YOP: 6/1959-67/68, $275-300 with hardware. *Courtesy of Sharen and Al Creery.*

Lavabo: 3867, YOP: 6/1955-76, $175-185.
Courtesy of Sharen and Al Creery.

Back: Ivy Ball: 3757, YOP: 1957-67/68, $20-25; Ivy Ball: 3757, notice the difference in the crimps between these two items, YOP: 1957-67/68, $20-25; Ivy Ball: 3726, YOP: 6/1959-67/68, $20-25. Front: Violet Vase, 3754, YOP: 1960-67/68, $35-40; Violet Vase: 3754, notice the difference in the crimps between these two items, YOP: 1960-67/68, $35-40.

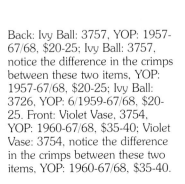

Planter, 8.5": 3697, YOP: 1966-79, $20-25; Planter, 10": 3799, YOP: 1960-78, $30-35.

Jardinière: 3898, YOP: 1975-78, $40-45; Jardinière, 6": 3996, YOP: 1952-69,
$20-25; Jardinière, 4": 3994, YOP: 1952-69, $10-12.

Bowl, Planter, 5.75": Made by Fenton, for their Old Virginia Glass Line, YOP: mid-1970s, $15-20.

Below:
Planter, Crescent: 3798, YOP: 6/1960-65, $40-45; Planter, Crescent: 3698, YOP: 1961-66, $55-65.

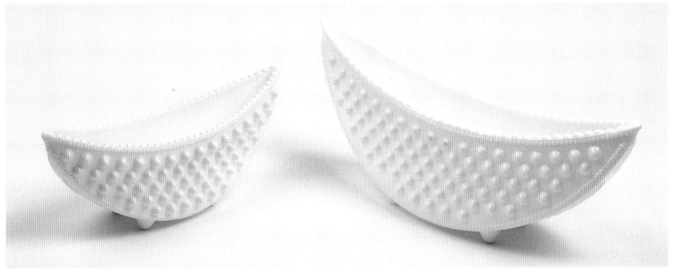

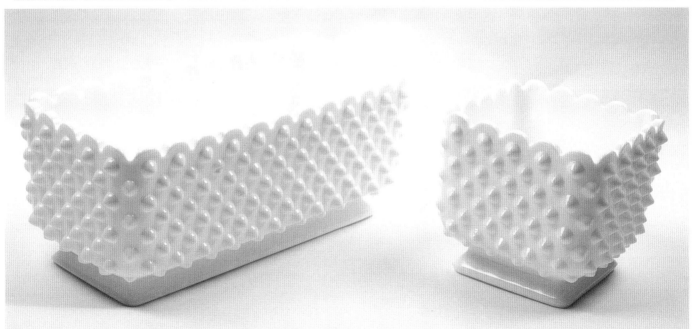

Planter, 9": 3690, YOP: 1962-76, $30-35; Planter, Square: 3699, YOP: 1961-81, $15-20.

Planter, Wall: 3836, YOP: 1956-6/56, $90-100.

Plates, 8": 3816, ruffled and straight edge, YOP: 1956-66, $30-35; Front/ Left: Plate, 8.5": 3912, YOP: 1955-56, $35-40.

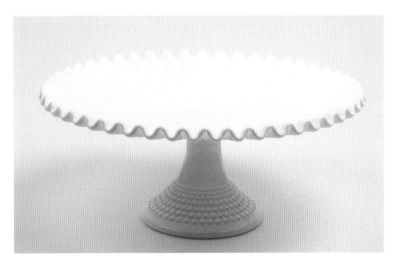

Cake Plate, Footed: 3913, YOP: 1956-89, $40-50.

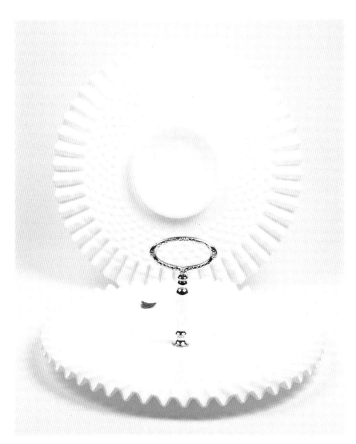

Back: Plate, 13.5": 3714, YOP: 6/1959-66, $65-75; Sandwich Tray: 3791, YOP: 1959-73, $60-65.

Boot: 3992, YOP: 1971-84, $15-20; Candy Box Slipper, Covered: 3700, YOP: 1971-84, $40-45; Slipper: 3995, YOP: 1952-89, $10-15.

Server, Two Tier: 3709, YOP: 1970-79, $60-65; Tidbit, Two Tier: 3794, YOP: 1959-83, $60-65.

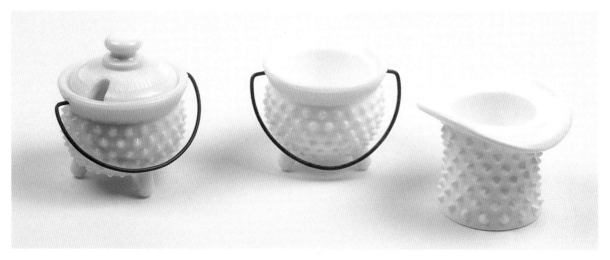

Hat, 2.5": 3991, YOP: 1952-56, 1961-69; Plain Hobbs, $150-175; Burred Hobbs, $15-20; Kettle: 3990, YOP: 1952-67/68, $15-20; Mustard Kettle: 3979, YOP: 1954-56, 6/1959-67, $20-30.

Toothpick Holder: 3895, YOP: 1971-86, $35-40; Toothpick Holder: 3795, YOP: 1966-84, $10-15.

Vase, Mini: 3855, YOP: 1952-67/68, $10-15.

Vase, Mini: 3855, YOP: 1952-67/68, $10-15; Vase, 5.5": 3656, YOP: 1962-73, $35-40; Vase, 3": 3853, YOP: 1952-84, $10-15; Vase, 4.5": 3854, YOP: 1952-89, $15-20; Vase, 5": 3850, YOP: 1970-83, $20-25.

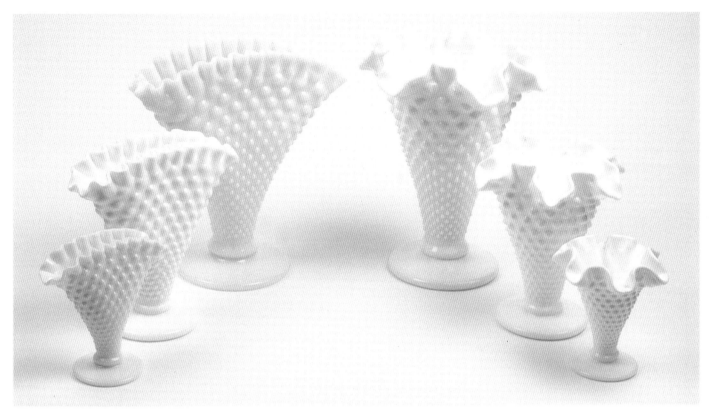

Vase, Fan, 4": 3953, YOP: 1952-71, $10-15; Vase, Fan, 6.25": 3957, YOP: 6/1953-71, $25-30; Vase, Fan, 8": 3959, YOP: 1956-71, $40-45; Vase, D.C., 8": 3958, YOP: 1956-77, $30-35; Vase, D.C., 6.25": 3956, YOP: 6/1953-78, $20-25; Vase, D.C., 4": 3952, YOP: 1952-84, $10-15.

Vase, Hand: 3355, YOP: 1992, $100+. *Courtesy of Sharen and Al Creery.*   Rear view of the 3355 Hand Vase.

Bowl: 3855, $10-15; Mini Bud Vase, UND. *Courtesy of Cindy and Rick Blais.*

Vase, Fan, 8": 3852, YOP: 1971-72, $150-175. *Courtesy of Sharen and Al Creery.*

Vase, 3 Toed: 3654, YOP: 1963-79, $15-20; Vase, 3 Toed, 12": 3658, YOP: 1967-68, $400-425. *Courtesy of Sharen and Al Creery.*

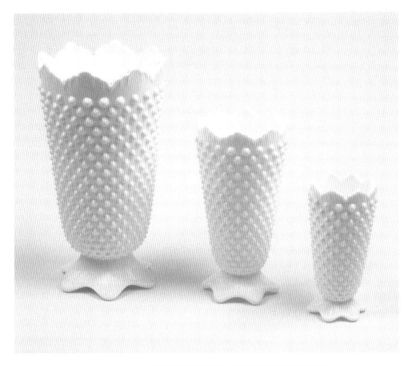

Vase, 9": 3659, YOP: 1962-73, $55-65; Vase, 7": 3657, YOP: 1962-76, $25-30; Vase, 5": 3655, YOP: 1962-76, $20-25.

Vase, 8": 3859, YOP: 1953-66, $125-150; Vase, 8": 3858, YOP: 1970-73, $66-70; Vase, 6": 3856, YOP: 1952-73, $35-40.

Vase, Handkerchief, 6": 3750, YOP: 6/1959-78, $20-25; Vase, Handkerchief: 3651, YOP: 1970, $45-55; Vase, Handkerchief: 3651, YOP: 1970, $45-55; Vase, Handkerchief, 9": 3855, YOP: 1977-78, $40-45.

Vase, Handkerchief: 3651, YOP: 1970, $45-55; Vase, Handkerchief: 3951, YOP: 1972-73, $50-55; Bud Vase: 3950, YOP: 1972-89, $15-20; Bud Vase: 3756, YOP: 1957-84, $15-20.

Vase, Tall Handkerchief: 3755, YOP: 1960-62/1971-87, $70-75; Vase, Tall Handkerchief: 3755, YOP: 1960-62/1971-87, $70-75; Vase, Medium: 3758, YOP: 6/1959-80, $30-35; Vase, Tall Footed: 3652, YOP: 1964-80, $45-55; Vase, Tall: 3759, YOP: 6/1959-80, $50-55; Vase, Footed: 3753, YOP: 6/1959-84, $30-35; Vase, Footed: 3753, YOP: 6/1959-84, $30-35; Pitcher Vase: 3760, YOP: 1960-76, $70-75.

Vase, 11": 3752, YOP: 1958-89, $45-55; Vase, 6": 3954, YOP: 1972-73, 1975-89, $25-30.

Vase, Tulip Crimp,
6.75": NIL, YOP: ???,
$25-30; Vase, 7.5": NIL,
YOP: ???, $25-30; Vase,
Footed, 4.75": NIL,
YOP: ???, $40-45; Vase,
Epergne Tulip: NIL,
YOP: ???, $40-45.

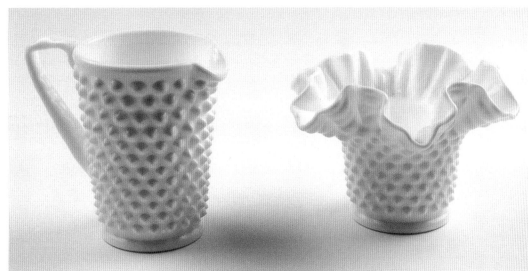

Pitcher: NIL, YOP: ???, $45-
55; Vase: NIL, YOP: ???, $20-
25. *Courtesy of Wanell and
Walt Jones.*

Syrup: 3660, YOP: 1987-89, $45-55;
Bell: 3067, YOP: 1987-89, $25-30; Vase,
8.5", YOP: 1992-95, $45-55. *Courtesy of
Bobbie & Harold Morgan.*

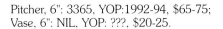

Pitcher, 6": 3365, YOP:1992-94, $65-75;
Vase, 6": NIL, YOP: ???, $20-25.

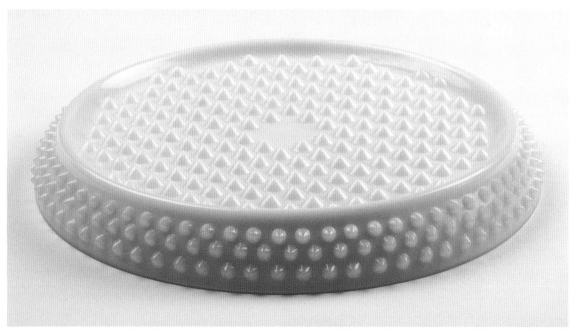

Tray (was to have been used for condiment set, but the hole wasn't adapted for drilling when it was made): $30-35.

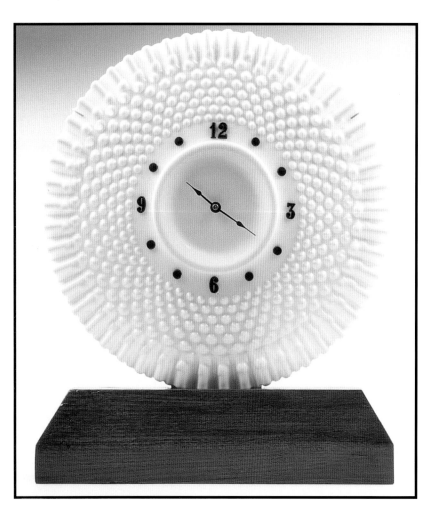

Wall Clock, 13": made from the 3714 Plate, $100-150.
Courtesy of Diane and Tom Rohow.

Lamp: made from the 3926 Bonbon, 3869 Oil Bottle, and the 3927 7" Bowl, $100-125.
Courtesy of Darcie Smith.

Hobnail Rose Pastel: 1954-1956, Turquoise Pastel: 1955-1958, Green Pastel: 1954-1955, Blue Pastel 1/1954-6/1954 Hobnail

The most popular line of Fenton's pastel colors had to be the Hobnail line, which accounts for the wide variety of pieces available. In 1954, Fenton introduced Rose Pastel along with Blue and Green Pastel. Blue and Green Pastel did not sell well and were gone by the end of the year, replaced by Turquoise, which lasted until 1959. (Rose Pastel was discontinued two years before.) Scarce pieces are any in Blue Pastel, the five piece epergne, hurricane lamp, and low candy in Rose and Green Pastel. In Turquoise, items to watch for are the cologne set, both epergnes, the low candy, squat jug, lavabo, and 5 oz. tumblers. Also known to exist are sherbets and water goblets in Turquoise. As the 1950s glassware becomes more collectible and demand rises, this is a pattern to keep an eye on.

Years of Production: Turquoise: 1955-1958 (unless noted); Rose Pastel: 1954-1956 (unless noted).

Item Description	Ware Number	Rose Pastel/ Blue Pastel	Green Pastel	Turquoise
Basket, 4.5"	3834	$55-65	$35-45	$35-45
Basket, 7"	3837	$55-65	$45-55	$45-55
Bonbon, 6"	3926	$10-15	$5-10	$5-10
Berry dish, sq.	3928	$15-20	$10-15	$10-15
Bowl, 9"	3924	$55-65	$35-45	$35-45
Bowl, 9", sq.	3929	$65-75	$35-45	$40-50
Candlestick	3974	$35-40 ea.	$30-35 ea.	$30-35 ea.
Candy jar, low	3883	$55-65	$35-45	$45-55
Candy jar, footed	3887	$65-75	$45-55	$55-75
Cologne bottle	3865			$75-85
Comport	3920	$40-45	$35-40	$35-40
Creamer, star crimped	3906	$35-40	$15-20	$25.-30
Epergne, footed, 5 pc.	3801	$300+	$400+	$300-350
Epergne	3801	$140-150	$100-125	$140-150
Lamp, hurricane	3998	$125-150	$100-125	
Jug, squat	3965			$90-100
Kettle	3990	$35-40	$25-30	
Lavabo	3867			$250-300
Oil	3869			$40-45
Powder jar	3885			$65-75
Cake plate, footed 13"	3913			$90-100
Shakers	3995			$55-65
Slipper	3995	$65-75	$55-65	$55-65
Sugar, star crimped	3906	$35-40	$15-20	$25-30
Tumbler, 5 oz.	3945			$15-20
Vase, 4", D.C.	3952	$10-15	$5-10	$10-15
Vase, 4.5, fan	3953	$15-20	$10-15	$15-20
Vase, 4.5", D.C.	3854	$35-40	$25.-30	$30-35
Vase, 5"	3850			$65-75
Vase, 8" fan, footed	3959			$65-75
Wall planter	3936			$135-150

Baskets, 4.5": 3834, in Turquoise, Rose Pastel, and Green Pastel. *See table for values.*

Basket, 7": 3837.

Bowl, 9" square: 3929.

BACK: Bowl, 9": 3924. FRONT: Bowl, square dessert: YOP: 1955-56; Bonbon, 6": 3926.

Cologne bottle: 3865; Powder jar: 3885; YOP:
TU: 1/1956-6/56. *Courtesy of Eileen and Dale
Robinson.*

Candy, Covered, Footed: 3887 in Rose
and Blue Pastel, YOP: RP: 1954.
Courtesy of Randy Clark Auctions.

Comport: 3920; Candy, Covered:
3883, YOP: RP: 1954; Candy,
Covered, Footed: 3887, YOP: RP:
1954.

69

Candlesticks, low: 3974; Epergne, mini: 3801.

Epergne, 5 piece: 3800 (consisting of a 3902 Comport, flower frog, and 3801 Epergne horns). *Author's Collection.*

Lamp, Hurricane: 3998 in Green Pastel, Blue Pastel, and Rose Pastel. *Courtesy of Alice and James G. Rose.*

Shakers: 3808, YOP: TU: 1955-56; Sugar, star crimped: 3906; Creamer,
star crimped: 3906, YOP: TU: 1955-56; Oil: 3869, YOP: TU: 1955-57.

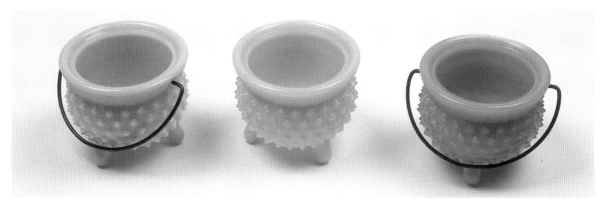

Kettle/bail (Match Holder): 3990 in Rose Pastel, Green Pastel, and Blue Pastel.

Jug, Squat: 3965; Tumbler, 5 oz.: 3945, YOP: TU: Both
1955-56. *Author's Collection.*

Lavabo: 3867. *Courtesy of Eileen and Dale Robinson.*

Slipper: 3995 in Blue Pastel, Rose Pastel, and Green Pastel, YOP: TU: 1955-56. *Author's Collection.*

Vase, 5": 3850; Not Pictured: Vase, 8" Footed Fan: 3939.

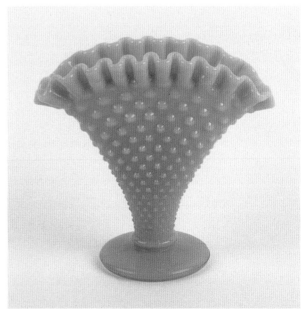

Vase, 4.5" Fan: 3854.

Royal Hobnail: SC: 1995

In 1995, during one of Fenton's brief issues of the regular Milk Glass Hobnail pattern, it was decided to also issue various pieces with a Clear Crest. This issue was dubbed Royal Hobnail. Although it has not been long since Royal Hobnail's introduction, these items seldom appear on the market.

Not Pictured: Royal Hobnail

Comport, 3314, $35-45.
Vase, footed, 6", 3357, $30-40.

Bonbon, Heart: 3733, YOP: 1995, $40-50.

Fairy Light, 3 piece: 1167, YOP: 1995, $75-85.

Epergne: 3701, $100-125. *Courtesy of Bobbie & Harold Morgan.*

Basket, 8.5": 3344, $45-55; Basket, Ftd.: 3345, $55-65

Lily Bowl: 3328, $35-45; Basket, Ftd.: 3345, $55-65; Cruet: 3363, $65-75; Fairy Light, 3 pc.: 1167, $75-85. *Courtesy of Bobbie & Harold Morgan.*

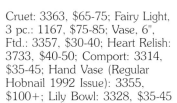

Cruet: 3363, $65-75; Fairy Light, 3 pc.: 1167, $75-85; Vase, 6", Ftd.: 3357, $30-40; Heart Relish: 3733, $40-50; Comport: 3314, $35-45; Hand Vase (Regular Hobnail 1992 Issue): 3355, $100+; Lily Bowl: 3328, $35-45

Jacqueline: MG: 1961

First made in 1960 in Opaline, Jacqueline was named for the new first lady of the United States, Jacqueline Kennedy. In 1961, Jacqueline was produced in Milk Glass and Overlay colors.

Not Pictured: Jacqueline

Sugar/Creamer, 9100 YOP: 1961 $25-30.
Salt/Pepper, 9106 YOP: 1961-7/62 $20-25.
Pansy Vase, 9150 1961 $10-15.

Basket, 10.5": 9139, YOP: NIL Late 1980s?, $40-45.

Pitcher: 9166, YOP: 1961, $35-45.
Courtesy of Norma and Melvin Lampton.

Vase, 6": 9156, YOP: 1961, $20-25.

Lace Edge: MG: ; RP: 1954-; BP/GP: 1954; Turquoise: 1955-

Throughout the course of the 1950s, Fenton made several different lace edge patterns, including the "C" Series, Scroll & Eye, and several other types of lattice edge type borders. Made not only in Milk Glass, but in all the Pastel colors also, some of these pieces are quite scarce in today's market. Watch for the Scroll & Eye Plate, as it served double duty for the Cranberry Polka Dot Butter Bottom.

Lacy Shell: 9030, YOP: TU: 1955-57, MI: 1955-63.

Plate, 12": 9012, YOP:
RP/MG: 1955-57.

Comport: 9021, YOP: GP/BP: 1954, RP: 1954-56, MG: 1955-59,
TU: 1955-54; Plate, 12": 9012, YOP: RP/MG: 1955-57; Comport,
"C" Series: 9029, YOP: BP/GP: 1954, RP: 1954-56, TU: 1955-56,
MG: 1952-63.

Plate, Ftd., "Scroll & Eye"
NIL, $45-55.;*Courtesy of
Cindy and Rick Blais.*

Item Description	Mould Number	Pastel Colors	MG	Item Description	Mould Number	Pastel Colors	MG
"C" Series				*Lattice Edge*			
Bowl, 8"	9026	$20-25	$10-15	Bowl	9031		$15-20
Comport, footed	9029	$25-30	$20-25	Bowl, 13" Oval			$20-25
Plate Planter	9099	$25-30	$10-15	Bowl, Flared	9023		$20-25
Plate, 9"	9019		$10-15	Banana Boat	9024	$35-40	
				Comport	9028		$30-35
Scroll/Eye				Comport, footed	9029		$20-25
				Plate 8"	9018		$10-15
Comport	9021	$25-30	$20-25	Plate, 11"	9011		$15-20
Bowl	9025	$20-25	$15-20	Plate 12"	9012	$25-30	$15-20
Plate	9015	$20-25	$10-15	Plate, footed	9013		$30-35
				Plate, footed	9017		$45-55
				Lacy Shell	9030	$25-30	$10-15

Lamb's Tongue 1954-1956

Lamb's Tongue, in Milk Glass, is almost impossible to find, particularly in any of the Pastel Colors. As of yet, I have seen only a few items in Milk Glass, and have yet to see one piece of this pattern in Rose Pastel!! Made only for two years, any item in this pattern is rare!

Years of Production: 4369 Oil Bottle, 4301 Creamer/Sugar: 1954 only, all colors; 4381 Candy Jar, 4303 Mayonnaise, 4306 Shakers: GP: 1954-55, BP: 1954 only, Turquoise: 1955 only.

Item	Ware #	Blue/ Pink Pastel	Green Pastel	Turquoise	Milk Glass
Candy jar	4381			$65-75	$65-75
Creamer	4301	$60-75	$50-55		$65-75
Mayonnaise	4303	$75-85	$45-55		$35-45
Oil bottle	4369	$300-350	$200-250		$150-175
Shakers	4306	$70-80	$55-65		$80-90
Sugar	4301	$60-75	$50-55		$65-75

Candy: 4381.

Oil Bottle: 4369. *Author's Collection.*

Bottles, Oil: 4369. *Courtesy of Betty and Ike Hardman.*

Shakers: 7001; Mayonnaise: 4303. *Courtesy of Betty Merrell.*

Mayonnaise: 4303.

Lamps

Many different lamps that Fenton produced in the 1980s in colors were also produced in Milk Glass. Most notable among them were the Poppies Lamps (which was also made in the satin colors), the Water Lily Student Lamp, the Roses Gone With The Wind (GWTW) Lamp, and the Roses Student Lamp.

Lamp, Poppy, 18": 9105, $250-300. *Courtesy of Sharen and Al Creery.*

Lamp, Poppy, GWTW, 24": $300-350. *Courtesy of Marilyn and Dick Trierweiler.*

Leaf: MG: ; RP: 1955-; GP/BP: 1954; Turquoise: 1955-

Over the years the 8" and 11" Leaf plate has enjoyed issues in many colors and treatments. First introduced in the 1930s in Jade and other Opaque colors, it was later introduced in Blue, Topaz, and French Opalescent. In the 1950s it was introduced in the Pastel Milk Glass colors, as well as White Milk Glass.

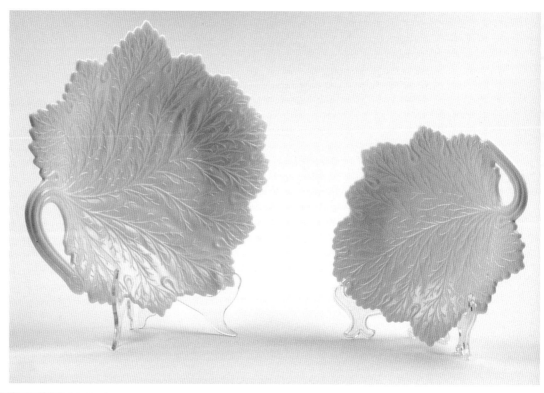

Leaf, 8": 5116, YOP: 1955-65, $10-15; Leaf, 11": 5118, YOP: 1955-65, $15-20. *Courtesy of Diane and Tom Rohow.*

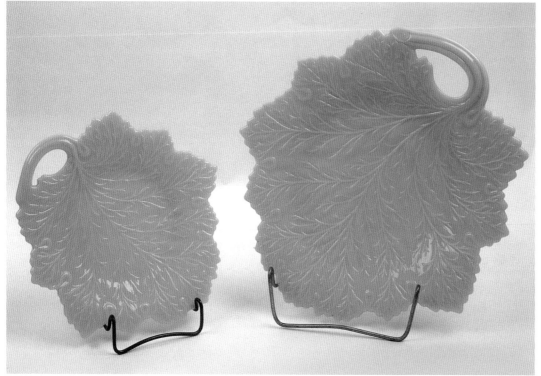

Leaf, 8": 5116, YOP: RP/TU: 1955-57, $30-40; Leaf, 11": 5118, YOP: RP/TU: 1955-57, $40-50.

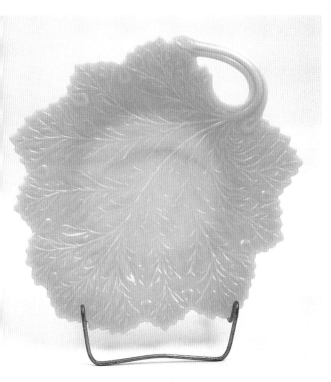

Leaf, 8": 5116, YOP: GP: 1954 NIL, $30-40.

Leaf Tidbit: 5196, YOP: RP/TU: 1955-57, $85-95. *Courtesy of Millie Coty.*

Leaf Tidbit: 5196, YOP: 7/55-65, $30-40. *Courtesy of JR Antiques.*

Miscellaneous Items

Over the years, Fenton has produced many unique items that do not fall into any large pattern. I have attempted to list them here. Keep in mind that many of these items, including the Grape & Cable Tobacco Jar, the Bathroom Set, and the Boudoir Lamp, are considered scarce to rare.

Not Pictured: Milk Glass

Basket, 4", 7331, YOP: 1953-55, 25-30.
Bathroom Set, 7302, YOP: 1955-56, $125-150.
Book End, Planter, Quilted, 5595, YOP: 6/1952-54, $35-45 each.

Bowl, footed, 7328, YOP: 1952-56, $35-40.
Boudoir Lamp (one piece Fairy Lamp), 7390, YOP: 1954-55, $100-125.
Canasta Set, 5808, YOP: 1953-56, $45-55.
Cigarette Set, Quilted, 5508, YOP: 6/1952-57, $55-65.
Flower Pot/Saucer, 7299, YOP: 1952-62, $15-20.
Bud Vase, 6", 7348, YOP: 1955-7/56, $10-15.
Bud Vase, 6.5", 7349, YOP: 1955-7/56, $10-15.
Vase, Handled, 7", 7251, YOP: 7/1955-7/56, $20-25.
Vase, 8.5", 7255, YOP: 7/1955-7/56.

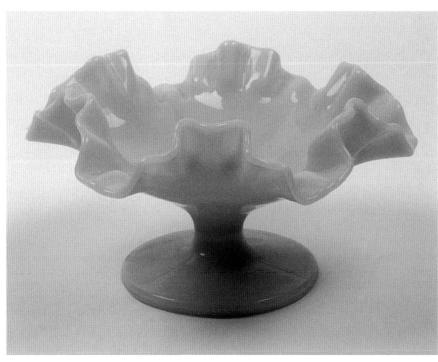

Comport: 7328, YOP: MG: 1952-58, BP/GP: 1954, RP: 1954-55, MG: $15-20, Pastel Colors: $25-30.

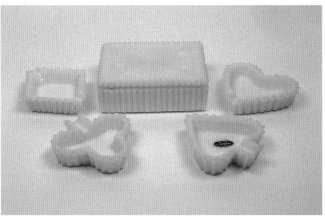

Ashtray, Diamond: 5876, Mirted, $5-10; Ashtray, Club: 5875, Mirted, $5-10; Cigarette Box: 5889, Mirted, $30-35; Ashtray, Spade: 5878, Mirted, $5-10; Ashtray, Heart, Mirted, $5-10; YOP: All 1952-53. *Courtesy of Fran and Bill Ersham.*

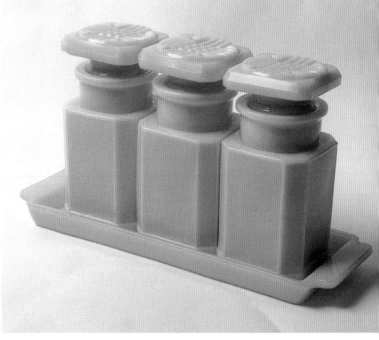

Bathroom Set: 7302, YOP: BP: 1954, GP: 1954-55, $200-250. *Author's Collection.*

Wild Strawberry Candy Box: 9088, YOP: 1969-70, $35-40.

Grape/Cable Tobacco Jar: 9188, YOP: 1969, $55-65.

Fairy Lamp, 1 piece: 7390, YOP: RP/GP/BP: 1954, $150-200.

Picture Frame/Easel: 9490, YOP: 1975, $15-20.
Courtesy of Diane and Tom Rohow.

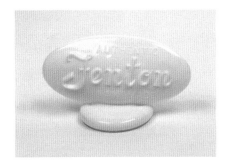

Logo 9499, YOP: ???, NIL $40-45. *Courtesy of Cindy and Rick Blais.*

Jug, 9": 7264, YOP: MG: 7/55-7/56, $20-25. TU: 1955-56, $40-45.

Clusterette, 4 piece: 7002, YOP: 6/1952-53, $20-25.

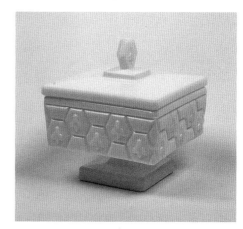

Honey Box: 9080, $20-25. *Courtesy of Diane and Tom Rohow.*

Hex Bowl: 8226, YOP: 1969-70, $25-35.

Vase: 8253, Vessel of Gems, YOP: 1968, $30-35

Top Hat, 7": 1923, $20-25.

Planter: 8299, YOP: 1969, $40-45.

Punch Ladle: 9527, $45-55.

Vase, Mini Hand #37: YOP: Circa 1942, $40-45.

Bud Vase, 6": 7348, YOP: BP/GP 1954, $20-25; RP: 1954-56, $25-35; MG: 1955-7/56, $10-15.

Vase, 4": 7352, $15-20; Vase, 3": 7351, YOP: 1953-7/57?, $10-15. *Courtesy of Diane and Tom Rohow.*

Vase, 4": 9426, $20-25. Made for the A. L. Randall Co.

Vase, 8", Wheat: 5858, $30-40.
Courtesy of Vickie Ticen.

Mandarin Vase: 8251, YOP: 1969- , $45-55; Empress Vase: 8252, YOP: 1969-, $45-55. *Courtesy of Norma and Melvin Lampton.*

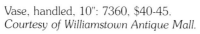

Vase, handled, 10": 7360, $40-45. *Courtesy of Williamstown Antique Mall.*

Vase, 12": 7364, $65-75; Vase, 10", 2 Handled: 7360, $75-85.

Regency: 1983 MI

Regency was made in 1983 off of moulds that Fenton had purchased from the old McKee Glass Company. Regency, though not in the Fenton line for long, makes a very striking table setting.

Not Pictured: Regency

Nut Dish, footed, 8622, $10-15.
Bowl, Cupped, 6", 8623, $15-20.
Relish, 8", 8640, $15-20.

Basket, 10": 8635, YOP: 1983, $20-25.

Comport, Footed: 8628, YOP: 1983, $10-15.
Courtesy of Diane Rohow.

Rose: MG: 1967-1976

Rose was another pattern inspired by an item that Frank Fenton bought at an antique show. Ironically, later on, Fenton bought several moulds from the U.S. Glass Company in Glassport, Pennsylvania, in this pattern. One item produced from these moulds, that was made in the regular Rose line, was the Large Oval Candy Box.

Rose is a very striking pattern, with small embossed Rose Buds seeming to pop from the sides of the items. Many people have started to collect Rose in both Milk Glass and the other colors in which it was produced.

Difficult items to find in Rose are the covered candy, 4" Oval Bowl, Soap Dish, Bathroom Tumbler, and the Shakers.

Not Pictured: Rose

Ash Tray, 9271, YOP: 1967-71, $15-20.
Bowl, 9.5", D.C., 9225, YOP: 1967-71, $25-30.
Candy Box, Covered, 9284, YOP: 1967, $30-35.
Ring Tree, 9299, YOP: 1967, $10-15.

Basket, 9": 9235, YOP: 1967-76, $35-40.

Bowl, 7": 9224, YOP: 1967-72, $20-25. *Courtesy of Norma and Melvin Lampton.*

Soap Dish: 9216, YOP: 1967-69, $10-15; Ashtrays w/Holder: 9210, $20-25; Tumbler, Bathroom: 9242, $15-20. *Courtesy of Bobbie & Harold Morgan.*

Vase, 9" Bud: 9256, YOP: 1970-76, $10-15; Candy: 9282, YOP: 1965-76, $30-35; Comport: 9222, YOP: 1965-76, $20-30; Bowl, Oval, 4": 9251, YOP: 1967-69, $30-35.

Sugar/Creamer: 9203, YOP: 1967-73, $20-25 each; Comport, D.C.: 9223, YOP: 1967-76, $15-20; Salt/Pepper: 9206, YOP: 1967-73, $25-30.

Candleholder: 9270, YOP: 1967-72, $15-20.

Bowl, Oval, 4": 9251, YOP: 1967-69, $30-35; Goblet: 9246, YOP: 1967-68, $20-25; Candlesticks: 9270, YOP: 1967-72, $15-20 ea; Vase, Handkerchief: 9254, YOP: 1970-71, $15-20; Bud Vase: 9256, YOP: 1970-76, $10-15.
Courtesy of Bobbie & Harold Morgan.

Lamp, Student, 19": 9208, $100-125.
Courtesy of Betty and Ike Hardman.

89

Silver Crest: SC: 1942-1990s

The only Fenton pattern to have a longer run in Milk Glass than the Hobnail pattern is Silver Crest. First introduced in 1941 as Crystal Crest, with an extra applied ring of white on each item, the line was soon revamped by leaving the white ring off and applying only the crystal ring. After that time, Fenton called the pattern Silver Crest. Under that name, it enjoyed a long and healthy life, with many items being introduced and discontinued year by year.

Silver Crest production slowed in the 1980s, as it did with Milk Glass Hobnail; however, in the 1990s several different Hand Painted patterns were developed using Silver Crest, and a small number of regular Silver Crest items were produced.

Scarce pieces in Silver Crest are any of the Beaded Melon #711 items (due to the fact that most were only in production for one year). The only items in the #711 Beaded Melon line that are somewhat common are the 6" Vase, in both the Jack in the Pulpit Crimp and Double Crimp, and the 6" Jug. These two items were produced on through the 1950s and 1960s, being discontinued in the early 1970s.

In the 1960s Fenton developed the Spanish Lace pattern into a complete Silver Crest Line. Previously, Spanish Lace had been used only on Bowls and Cake Plates in the 1950s. The Spanish Lace Silver Crest line featured several Baskets, Bowls, and Vases, along with a Cake Plate that was a smaller version of the one produced during the 1950s.

In the 1990s, as the chemicals used in making Milk Glass proved destructive to the day tanks, Silver Crest and Hobnail were both reduced to limited, periodic issues. One 1990s pattern that has caught the collector's eye is the Elizabeth pattern. Elizabeth incorporated items from the Paisley Line, manufactured in Milk Glass with

Silver Crest, and then sold both painted with a small deep blue floral decorations or left unpainted. Other embossed patterns, such as the Daffodils Vase and the Empress Comport, were produced in Silver Crest at this time. In the late 1990s, other plain shapes in the Fenton line were produced in Silver Crest and then painted with the Morning Mist pattern. Some of these shapes have escaped being painted, and appear from time to time.

One type of a crimp that appeared briefly during the early 1940s on Silver Crest has proven quite popular with collectors. Some people have christened it the Deco Crimp, as it is very streamlined, with either a very loose crimp or no crimp at all. Items appear in Deco Crimp from time to time, but are still considered scarce.

In the following pictures, I have arranged the items from the Fenton regular mould numbers first. These are the items which were used after 1952, when Fenton abandon their old ware number system for their present numbering system. Some of these items were in the Silver Crest line prior to 1952. When this is the case, they will also be shown also in the next section, with the earlier ware numbered items that Fenton produced in Silver Crest from 1942-1952. They will be identified with their ware number, and also with the mould number used for that item after 1952. In the next section are items that were in the #711 Beaded Melon line, which was made from 1949-1950. Following that are different embossed items made in Silver Crest, including Spanish Lace and the Elizabeth items from the 1990s. In the finial Silver Crest section are the Deco Crimp items produced in the early 1940s.

Not Pictured: 1952-1985

Bonbon, 2 Tiered, 7497, $35-45.
Epergne, 3 Pc., 7200, YOP: 1956-6/59, $125-150.
Tidbit, 2 Tired, 7297, YOP: 1952-6/54, $45-55.
Tidbit, 3 Tired, 7298, YOP: 1952-6/54, $55-65.
Tidbit, 3 Tired, 7397, YOP: 1956-59, $65-75.

Ashtray: 7377, YOP: 1960-64, $45-55.

Basket, 7": 7237, YOP: 1952-86, $45-55; Basket, 5": 7236, YOP: 1952-57 (later 7436, YOP: 1968/69-77), $45-55.

Basket, 7": 7337, YOP: ???, $40-45; Basket, Divided, 8": 7339, YOP: 1958-1959, $125-150; Basket, 6.5": 7336, YOP: 1957-63, 1970-86, $35-40.

Basket, 12": 7234, YOP: 6/1956-84, $90-110.

Basket, 13": 7233, YOP: 1952-, $125-150.
Courtesy of Marilyn and Dick Trierweiler.

Basket, Deep, 11": 7434, YOP: 1975-77, $100-125. *Courtesy of Marilyn and Dick Trierweiler.*

Bonbon, 5.5": 7225, YOP: 1952-84, $10-15; Bonbon, Handled: 7498, YOP: 1970-86, $20-25; Bonbon, 8": 7428, 6/1958-79, $25-30.

Shrimp/Dip: 7403, YOP: 1962-74, $100-125. (This price reflects the item with the Metal Toothpick Holder!). *Courtesy of Randy Bradshaw.*

Bottom:
Bowl, 6": 682, $25-30; Bowl, Soup: 7320, YOP: 1952-55, $30-35; Dessert, Deep: 7221, YOP: 1952-61, $15-20; Dessert, Low: 7222, YOP: 1952-64, $15-20.

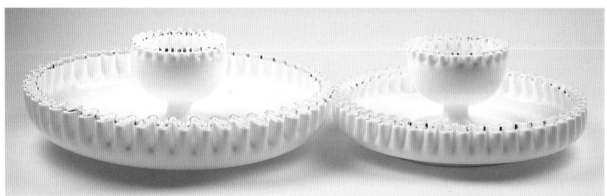

Left:
Chip 'n' Dip: 7402, YOP: 1975, $85-95; Chip/Dip: 7303, YOP: 1957-66, $85-95.
Courtesy of Randy Bradshaw.

Bowl, 7": 7227, YOP: 1952-80, $25-30; Bowl, 8.5": 7338, YOP: 1957-6/62, $45-65.

Bowl, 9.5": 7423, YOP: 1970-75, $40-45.

Bowl, D.C., 11.5": 7321, YOP: 1958-83, $50-60; Bowl Salad, 10": 7220, YOP: 1952-55, $50-60.

Bowl, Serving: 7335, YOP: 1955, $65-75.

Bowl, 10": 7224, YOP: 1952-71, $45-55.

Bowl; 13": 7223, YOP: 1952-71, $85-95.

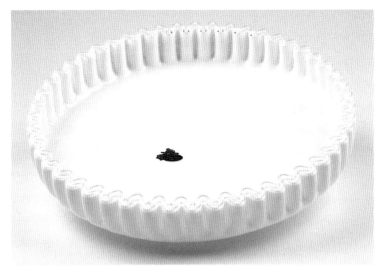

Bowl, 14": 7323, YOP: 1958-63, $85-95.

Bowl, Shallow: 7316, YOP: 6/1956-, $45-55.
Courtesy of Marilyn and Dick Trierweiler.

Bowl, Footed: 7328, YOP: 1958,
RARE!, $150-175. *Courtesy of
Marilyn and Dick Trierweiler.*

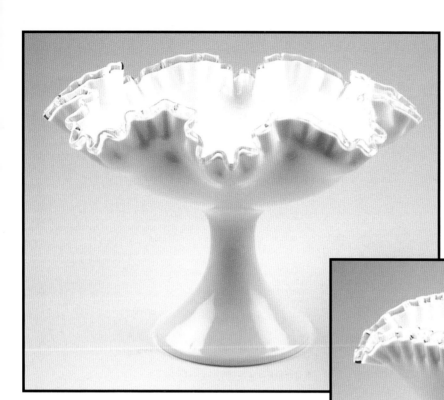

Bowl, Footed: 7427, YOP: 6/1959-75, $65-75.

Bowl, Footed Square: 7330, YOP: 1955-64, $75-85. *Courtesy of Marilyn and Dick Trierweiler.*

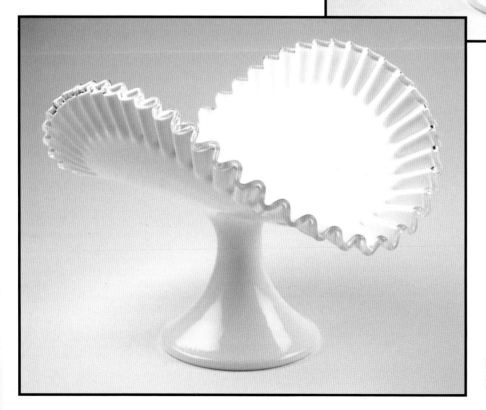

Bowl, Footed Banana: 7324, YOP: 1954-66, $100-125. *Courtesy of Marilyn and Dick Trierweiler.*

Candleholders, 6": 7474,
YOP: 6/1961-77, $35-40
each. Candleholders: 7272,
YOP: 1956-62, $35-45
each.

Candleholders: 7270, YOP:
1952-53, $35-45 each;
Candleholders: 7271, YOP:
1956-80, $20-25 each.

Cornucopia Candleholders: 7274, YOP: 1952-
66, $35-45 each.

Relish, Heart: 7333, YOP: 1955-86, $45-55; Relish, Divided: 7334, YOP: 1958-63, $45-55.

Mayonnaise Set: 7203, YOP: 6/1953-77, $40-50; Nut Dish, Footed: 7229, YOP: 1952-80, $30-35.

Nut Dish, Footed: 7229, YOP: 1952-80, $30-35; Comport; Low, Pie Crust Edge: YOP: ???, $45-55. Note the different shapes on the two nut dishes, yet both are 7229.

Creamer: 680, YOP: 1948, $90-100; Oil: 7269, YOP: 1952-54, $125-150; Creamer, Reeded Handled: 7261, YOP: 1952-7/56, $35-45; Sugar, Reeded Handled: 7231, YOP: 1952-7/56, $35-45; Salt/ Pepper: 7206, YOP: 1956-59, $100-125. *Courtesy of Marilyn and Dick Trierweiler.*

Salt/Pepper: 7205, marketed as Silver Crest, YOP: 6/1953-55, $150-200; Salt/Pepper: 7406, YOP: 1964-6/64, $175-200; Salt/Pepper: 7206, YOP: 1956-59, $100-125. *Courtesy of Randy Bradshaw.*

Bowl, Footed, 7.5": 7425, YOP: 1961-77, $35-45; Comport, Footed: 7228, YOP: 1952-80, $35-40; Comport, Footed: 7429, YOP: 1961-84, $35-40; Comport, Footed, Flared: 7430, YOP: 1961, $45-55.

Comport, Low Footed: 7329, YOP: 1954-77, $30-35.

Candy Boxes: 7280, YOP: 1956-64, $75-85. Notice the variation of the foot on the one to the left, and the center. Candy Box, Footed Spanish Lace: 3580, YOP: 1965-79, $65-75. *Courtesy of Marilyn and Dick Trierweiler.*

Pitcher, 5": 7363, YOP: 1969-71, $40-50. *Courtesy of Marilyn and Dick Trierweiler.*

Jug, 70 oz.: 7467, YOP: 6/1960-64, $350-400; Tumbler, Footed 7342, YOP: 1957-62, $75-80. *Courtesy of Marilyn and Dick Trierweiler.*

Punch Bowl: 7317, YOP: 1956-59, $400-450;
Pedestal for Punch Bowl: 7378, YOP: 1956-59,
$150-175; Punch Cups: 7247, YOP: 1956-59,
$15-20 each. *Courtesy of Randy Bradshaw.*

Punch Cup: 7247, YOP: 1956-59. Notice the ribbing on the inside
of the cups. *Courtesy of Randy Bradshaw.*

Pedestal for Punch Bowl: 7378, YOP: 1956-59,
$150-175. *Courtesy of Randy Bradshaw.*

Epergne: 7202, YOP: 6/1955-66, $100-125. *Courtesy of Marilyn and Dick Trierweiler.*

Epergne, 2 piece: 7301, YOP: 1957-59, $175-200. *Courtesy of Marilyn and Dick Trierweiler.*

Epergne, 4 piece: 7308, YOP: 6/1956-80, $125-150.

Epergne, 5 piece: 7305, YOP: 6/1956-77, $225-250. *Courtesy of Lynne and Gary Virden.*

Epergne, 2 piece: 7402, YOP: 1962-64, $500+. *Courtesy of Laurie and Richard Karman.*

Ivy Ball, Footed: 7232, YOP: 1956-58, $45-55; Hurricane Lamp: 7290, YOP: 1956-6/56, $250+. *Courtesy of Randy Bradshaw.*

Cake Plate, Footed: 7213, YOP: 1952-79, $65-75. *Courtesy of Marilyn and Dick Trierweiler.*

Cake Plate, Low Footed: 7312, YOP: 1954-55, $40-50. *Courtesy of Marilyn and Dick Trierweiler.*

Cup/Saucer, MG Handle, Flat: 7208, YOP: 1956-65, $25-35; Sherbets: 7226, YOP: 1952-64 (notice the different types and shapes of Sherbets, yet all have 7226 ware numbers), $25-30 each.

Cup/Saucer, Crystal Handle, Flat: 7208, YOP: 1953-56, $75-85; Cup/Saucer, Crystal Handle, Footed: 7209, YOP: 1952-53, $95-110; NP (**N**ot **P**ictured); Cup/Saucer, MG Handle, Footed: 7209, $35-45.

Back: Torte Plate, 16": 7216, YOP: 1954-, $65-75; Plate, 12.5": 7211, YOP: 6/1956-71, $45-50; Plate, 10.5": 7210, YOP: 1952, $40-45; Plate, 10": 7210, YOP: 1952-66, $40-45. Middle: Plate, 8.5": 7217, YOP: 1952-, $20-25; Plate, 6.5": 7219, YOP: 1952-64, $10-15. Front: Plate, 12": 7212, YOP: 1952-59, $45-50; Cup/Saucer, MG Handle, Flat: 7208, YOP: 1956-65, $60+. *Courtesy of Marilyn and Dick Trierweiler.*

Tidbit, 3 Tier: 7295, YOP: 6/1954-77, $45-95.

Tidbit, 2 Tier: 7394, YOP: 1958-75, $45-55. *Courtesy of Randy Bradshaw.*

Tidbit, 2 Tier: 7294, YOP: 6/1954-83, $45-55; Tidbit, 2 Tier: 7296, YOP: 1954-76, $45-55. *Courtesy of Randy Bradshaw.*

Sandwich Tray: 7291, YOP: 1959-80, $50-55.

Vase, 8": 7453, YOP: 1959-64, $45-55; Vase, 6": 7451, YOP: 1959-82, $30-40.

Vase, 10": 7450, YOP: 1959-6/59, $100-125; Vase, 7": 7455, YOP: 1959, $45-55; Vase, 8.5": 7458, YOP: 1959, $65-75. *Courtesy of Marilyn and Dick Trierweiler.*

Vase, 8", D.C.: 7258, YOP: 1952-66, $30-35; Vase, 12" Fan: 7262, YOP: 1956-66, $75-100; Vase, 4.5": 7254, YOP: 1954-72, $20-25. *Courtesy of Marilyn and Dick Trierweiler.*

Vase, 9": 7454, YOP: 1959-6/61, $75-85; Vase, 9": 7459, YOP: 1959-62, $65-75; Vase, 7": 7252, YOP: 1968-77, $60-70. *Courtesy of Marilyn and Dick Trierweiler.*

Vase, 6": 7256, YOP: 1954-58, $40-50. *Courtesy of Marilyn and Dick Trierweiler.*

Vase, 11": 7458, YOP: 1971-72, $80-90; Vase, 10": 7450, YOP: 1959-60, $75-85. *Courtesy of Marilyn and Dick Trierweiler.*

Vase, 6.5": 6058, YOP: 1958-62, $55-65.

Silver Crest - Early Ware Numbers: 1942-1952

Not Pictured: #711 Items

Basket, 10", 711, $125-150.
Rose Bowl, 5", 711, $65-75.
Jug, Squat, 711, $175-200.
Tumbler, 5 oz., 711, $65-75.
Vase, 5", 711, $45-55.
Vase, 5.5", 711, $30-40.

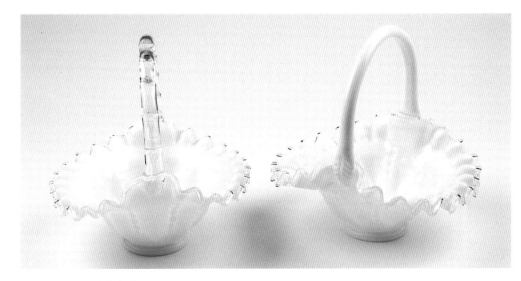

Basket, 7", with Clear Handle: 711, $75-85; Basket, 7", with Milk Glass Handle: 711, $75-85. *Courtesy of Marilyn and Dick Trierweiler.*

Bowl, 7": 711, $25-30.

Jug, 6": 711, $45-55; Puff Box: 711, $45-55; Vanity Bottle: 711, $55-65.

Rose Bowl, 4": 711, $55-65; Bottle, Vanity, 5.5": 711, $75-85. *Courtesy of Marilyn and Dick Trierweiler.*

Candy, Covered: 711, $75-85. *Courtesy of Lynne and Gary Virden.*

Vase, 9": 711 (notice the difference in beads on this vase as oppose to the 9" Vase in the previous picture), $65-75. *Courtesy of Gary and Lynne Virden.*

Jug, 9": 711, $100-110; Jug, 5.5": 711, $45-55; Creamer, 4": 711, $75-85; Jug, 8": 711, $125-150. *Courtesy of Marilyn and Dick Trierweiler.*

Vase, 4": 711, $25-35; Vase, 6": 711 (later 7156, 6" D.C. Vase, YOP: 1952-71), $30-35; Vase, Mini Bud, Jack in the Pulpit Crimp: 711, $30-40; Vase, 6": 711, $30-40; Vase, 6" Tulip: 7157, YOP: 1952-56, $35-45; Vase, 8": 711, $75-85; Vase, Mini Bud: 711, $30-40; Vase, 9": 711, $65-75; Vase, Mini Bud: 711, $30-40.

Not Pictured: 1942-1952 Items

Creamer, 192, $75-85.
Vase, 6", 192, $25-30.

Basket, 4" Footed: 36, YOP: 1943-47, $75-90; Basket, 7": 203 (later 7237), YOP: 1942-52, $35-45; Basket, 4", Milk Glass Handle: 1924, YOP: 1943-52, $55-65; Basket, 4": 1924, YOP: 1942-52, $55-65. *Courtesy of Marilyn and Dick Trierweiler.*

Basket, 4", Footed, Milk Glass Handle: 36, YOP: 1943-47, $75-90. *Courtesy of Lynne and Gary Virden.*

Basket, 10": 201, YOP: 1946-47, $100-125.

Basket, 5". 680 (later 7/236), YOP: 1949-52, $45-55.

Basket, 10": 192, YOP: 1942-48, $100-125.

Basket, 13": 1523 (later 7233), YOP: 1942-52, $150-175. *Courtesy of Randy Bradshaw.*

Creamer: 37, $200+; Basket: 37, $275+; Vase: 37, $100-125. YOP: All 1942.

Bonbon, Tri-crimp: 36, $15-20; Bonbon, D.C.: 36, $15-20.

Dessert/Finger Bowl: 202, YOP: 1948-52 (later 7221, YOP: 1952-62), $15-20.

Bowl, 8.5": 205, YOP: Circa 1942, $25-35.

Bowl, 7": 203, $20-30; Vase, 4": 203, $20-30; Vase, 3": YOP: ???, $30-40 RARE; Lamp shade, 7": 203, $20-30.

Bowl, 8.5": 680, YOP: 1949-52, $20-30. *Courtesy of Lynne and Gary Virden.*

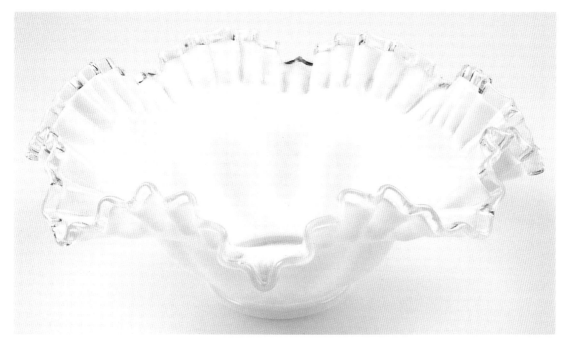

Bowl, 10": 192, YOP: 1942-47, $40-50.

Bowl, 10": 1522, YOP: 1942-52, $45-55.

Bowl, 13": 1523, YOP: 1943-52 (later: 7223, YOP: 1952-71), $85-95.

Powder: 192, $45-55; Bottle, 7": 192, $65-75; Bottle, Large: 192A, $65-75; Powder/Candy: 192, $65-75; Bottle, Small: 192A, $35-45; Bottle, 7": 192, $65-75. YOP: All: 1942-47. *Courtesy of Randy Bradshaw.*

Bottle, 5": 192, $45-55; Bottle, 7": 192, $65-75; Powder/Candy: 192, $65-75; Bottle, 7": 192, $65-75; Bottle, Small: 192A, $35-45; Powder: 192, $45-55; Bottle, Small: 192A, YOP: 1942-47, $35-45. *Courtesy of Marilyn and Dick Trierweiler.*

Bottle, Tall: 192 Turned Out (Special Order, Made for Abels Wasserberg Co. for decorating); Bottle, Small: 192A. Keep in mind that when these bottles were sold without stoppers, the short ones were classified as Candlesticks and the tall ones were listed as Bud Vases. Prices for these are about half of the price for examples with stoppers. Also, the examples that were sold as Bud Vases and Candlesticks were not ground in the neck, where the stoppers fit into the bottle. Left: $55-65 with stopper. Right: $35-45. *Courtesy of Lynne and Gary Virden.*

Epergne, Block/Vase: 1522, YOP: 1942-47, $150-175.

Candle Holders: 680, $50-75 each, rare.

Candleholder, bottom side: notice that the Silvertone pattern had not yet been removed from this mould.

Comport: 680, YOP: 1942-52, $30-40. (Piece pictured is crystal crest; price reflects silver crest).

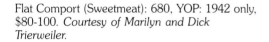

Flat Comport (Sweetmeat): 680, YOP: 1942 only, $80-100. *Courtesy of Marilyn and Dick Trierweiler.*

Creamer: 1924. Notice the Milk Glass Handle on this example and the clear handle on the creamer in the next picture. Examples are also known in this shape with a clear handle and no crest. YOP: 1942-47, $75-85. *Courtesy of Alice and James Rose.*

Top Hat: 1924, YOP: 1942-52, $30-40; Top Hat, 9": 1922, YOP: 1942-44, $150-175. *Courtesy of Randy Bradshaw.*

Top Hat: 1924, YOP: 1942-52, $30-40; Top Hat, 9": 1922, YOP: 1942-44, $150-175; Top Hat, 7": 1923 (later 7923), YOP: 1942-52, $45-55. Vase, 4": 1924, $20-30.

Jug, 5.5": 192, $35-45; Jug, 6": 192, YOP: 1942-47, $35-45.

Jug, 8": 192, $85-95. Price reflects Glossy version, not Satinized.

Left:
Jug, 9": 192A, $65-75.

Planter, 3 Tier: 680, YOP: 1950-52, $65-75. *Courtesy of Lynne and Gary Virden.*

Jug, Squat: 192, $180-200.

Vase, 4.25" Fan: 36 (later 7355, YOP: 1952-57), $25-30; Vase, 4.25" JIP: 36; Vase, 4.25" D.C.: 36 (later 7354, YOP: 1952-66), $20-25. YOP: All 1942-52.

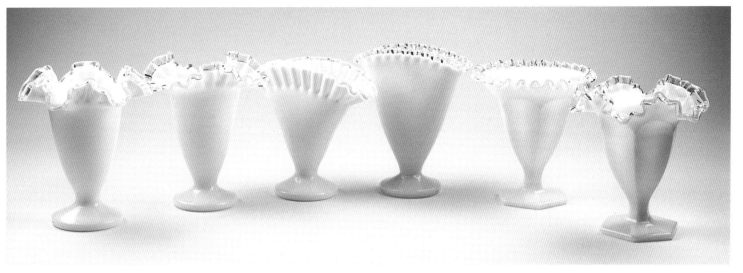

Vase, 6.25" D.C.: 36 (later 7356, YOP: 1952-66), $25-30; Vase, 6.25" Tri-Crimp: -6, $25-30; Vase, 6.25" Fan: 36; (later 7357, YOP: 1952-56), $35-40; Vase, 6.25" Fan: 36, $35-40. (Notice the variation in the shape of this vase and the previous example.) Vase, 6.25, Pie crust crimp: early 36 with slab sides; $25-30; Vase, 6.25" D.C.: early 36 with slab sides, $25-30. YOP: All Except for Slab Sided Vases, 1942-52; Slab Sided Vases, 1942 only.

Vase, 5": 201, $25-30; Vase, 4.5", D.C.: 203, $20-25; Vase, 4.5" Tri-crimp: 203, $20-25. YOP: All 1942-52.

Vase, 5": 192, YOP: 1942-47, $40-45.

Vase, 9": 192A, $35-45.
Vase, 8": 192, $35-45;
Vase, 5.5", Pie Crust Crimp: 192, $20-25; Vase, 5.5", JIP Crimp: 192, $20-25. YOP: All 1942-47. *Courtesy of Randy Bradshaw.*

Vase, 8", Flared: 573, $40-50; Vase, 8", Flared with Rolled Crimp: 573, $55-65; Vase, 8", Fan: 573, $45-55; Vase, 8", D.C.: 573, $40-50; Vase, 8", Flared: 573, $40-50. (Notice the difference in the crimps on the first and last vase!) YOP: All 1942-43. *Courtesy of Marilyn and Dick Trierweiler.*

Vase, 11": 3517, $55-65. Vase, 6": 3517, YOP. 1944-47, $35-45.

Vase, Hand, 10": 193, $175-200.
Courtesy of Alice and James Rose.

Spanish Lace Silver Crest

Basket, 10": 3537, YOP: 1968/69-79, $100-125; Basket, 8.5": 3538, YOP: 1973-86, $70-80. *Courtesy of Marilyn and Dick Trierweiler.*

Bell: 3567, YOP: 1973-86, $30-40.

Comport, Footed: 3522, YOP: 1975-86, $35-40; Candy Box, Footed: 3580, YOP: 1965-79, $65-75.

Candleholders: 3570, YOP: 1967-86, $20-25 each; Bowl, 9": 3524, YOP: 1968/69-86, $40-50.

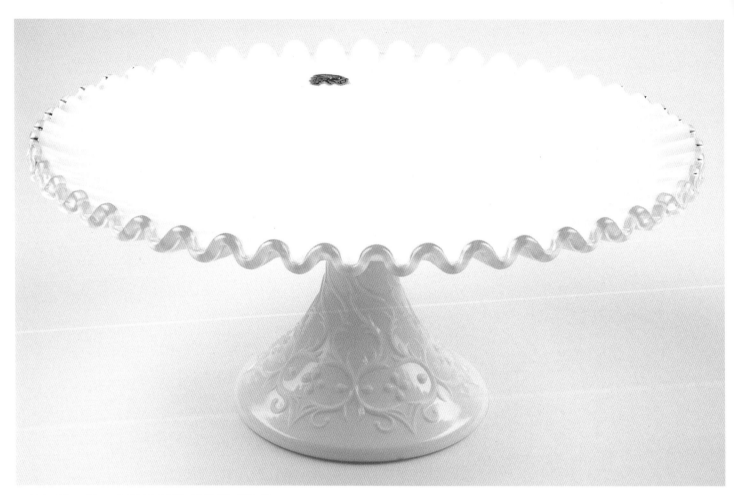

Cake Plate, Footed: 3510, YOP: 1962-86, $55-65.

Salt/Pepper: 3508, YOP: 1965-, $90-100.
Courtesy of Marilyn and Dick Trierweiler.

Vase, 8": 3551, YOP: 1967/68-86, $50-60; Vase, 4": 3554,
YOP: 1973-79, $20-25.

Miscellaneous Silver Crest

Banana Bowl, Ribbed: 5824, YOP: 1957-67/68, $45-55. *Courtesy of Marilyn and Dick Trierweiler.*

Back: Cake Plate, 13", Low, Footed, Ribbed: 5813, YOP: 1954-86, $35-45; Bowl, 11", Ribbed: 5823, YOP: 1958-67/68, $40-50.

Bowl, 10", Ribbed: 1522, YOP: ???, $75-85. *Courtesy of Marilyn and Dick Trierweiler.*

Epergne, Diamond Lace: 4801, YOP: 1992, $150-200.

Vase, Wheat D.C.: 5858, YOP: 1983-84, $55-65; Vase, Wheat: 5858, YOP: 1983-84, $55-65.

1990s Silver Crest

Basket, Paisley, 8.5": 6730, $35-45; Bowl, 7": $20-30. *Courtesy of Lynne and Gary Virden.*

Bells, Paisley: 6761, $20-25. (Note the difference in the crimp.)

Basket, Paisley, 8.5": 6730, $35-45; Comport, Empress: 9229, $30-35.

Bowl, 10": YOP: Circa 1990s, $30-40.

Plate, 12": 6710, $35-40. *Courtesy of Lynne and Gary Virden.*

Jardinières. (Notice the difference in the crimp.)

Vase, Melon; Basket, Melon, 8.75": 3132, $30-40.

Lamp, Double Student, Medallion Shade: $150-200.
Courtesy of Lynne and Gary Virden.

Lamp, Rose, GWTW, 23": 9219, YOP: 1992, $300-
350. *Courtesy of Linda and John Flippen.*

Pitcher, Sandwich: 9666, $35-40. *Courtesy of Lynne and Gary Virden.*

Lamp, 18", Student: 6505, $175-200; Vase, 10.5": 3240, $30-40. YOP: Both 1998.

Basket, 8", Ribbed: 6833, $35-45; Pitcher, 6": 4566, $25-30; Bell: 4769, $20-25; Vase, 10.5": 3240, $30-40; Basket, 5": 6530, $25-35. YOP: All 1998. These items were supposed to have been decorated with the Morning Mist decoration. As in all such patterns, there are a number of items that, for one reason or another, escape decoration!

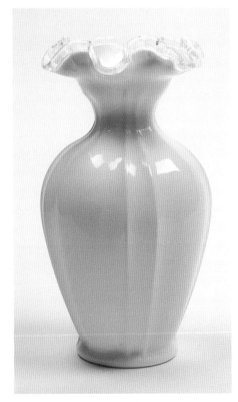

Vase, 7", Ribbed: 1683, $30-40. *Courtesy of Lynne and Gary Virden.*

Vase, Daffodils, 7.75": 9752, $35-40; Vase, Roses, 6.5": 9252, $35-40.

Pitcher, Apple Tree: 6575, $125-150; Vase, Apple Tree: $100+;
Vase, Apple Tree: $100+. *Courtesy of Marilyn and Dick Trierweiler.*

Deco Silver Crest

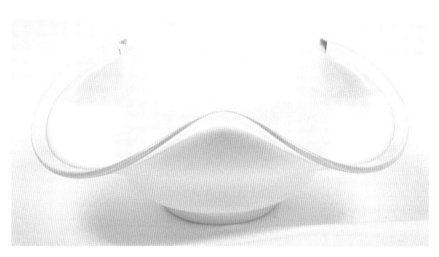

Bowl, 10", Tri-crimp: 1522, $80-90. *Courtesy of Lynne and Gary Virden.*

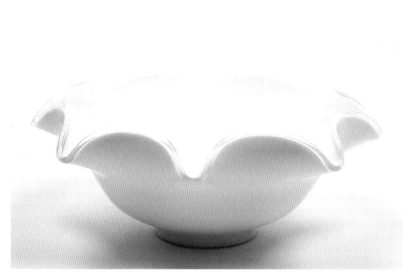

Bowl, 10": 1522, $80-90. *Courtesy of Lynne and Gary Virden.*

Vase, 4", Jack in the Pulpit Crimp: 36, $55-65. *Courtesy of Marilyn and Dick Trierweiler.*

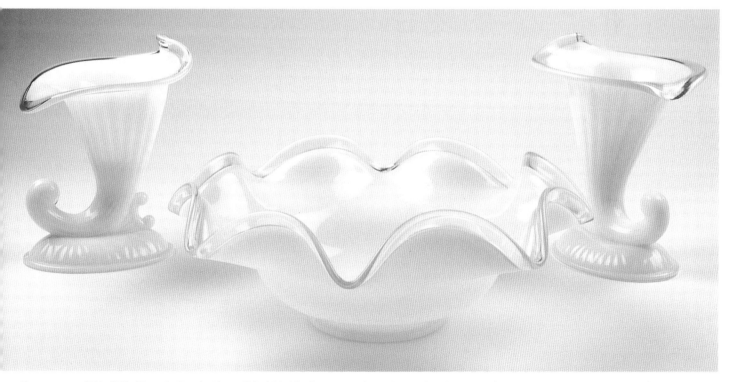

Cornucopia: 951, $55-65 each; Bowl, 10": 1522, $80-90. *Courtesy of Marilyn and Dick Trierweiler.*

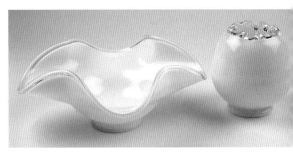

Bowl, 8.5": 205, $75-85; Rose Bowl, 4": 203, $65-75

Vase, 6": 1925, $75-85; Vase, 8": 573, $80-90.

Vase, 4": 36, $45-55

Vase, 6", Slab Sides: 36, $55-65; Vase, 4": 36, $30-40; Vase, 6": 36, $45-55; Vase, Fan, 4": $45-55.

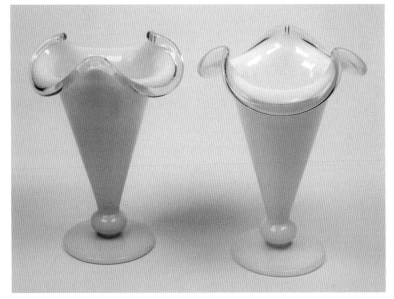

Vases, 8": 573, $80-90 each. *Courtesy of Marilyn and Dick Trierweiler.*

Vase, 6", Slab Sides: 36, $55-65. *Courtesy of Lynne and Gary Virden.*

Crystal Crest: 1941

Crystal Crest was the forerunner of Silver Crest. First introduced in 1941, it was made with a Milk Glass body that had a clear ring applied to it and another ring of opal applied to the clear. It proved difficult and costly to make and as soon discontinued. Crystal Crest was revamped and released as the more successful Silver Crest.

Most any item in Crystal Crest is scarce. Rare items include any baskets, pitchers (including the #1353 Pitcher pictured in my *Fenton Rarities* book), the vanity set, and the hand vase.

Not Pictured: Crystal Crest

Basket, footed, 4", 36, $175-200.
Basket, 10", 201, $200-250.
Basket, 13", 1523, $350+.
Dessert/Finger, Bowl, 202, $35-45.
Bowl, 8.5", 205, $85-95.

Bowl, 13", 1523, $150-175.
Bottle, Small, 192A, UND.
Bottle, Large, 192A, UND.
Bottle, 5", 192, UND.
Candle, Holder, 192, UND.
Candle, Holder, 680, $150+.
Candle, Holder, 1523, $100+ each.
Candy, 192, UND.
Comport, 206, $95-110.
Creamer, Mini, 36, $175-200.
Creamer, 192, $125-150.
Creamer, 1924, $100+.
Jug, 192, 5.5", $125-150.
Jug, 8", 192, $200-225.
Jug, 9", 192A, $175-200.
Powder, 192, UND.
Vase, 5", 201, $75-85.
Vase, 6", 1923, $75-85.
Vase, 9", 192A, $80-90.
Hand, Vase, 10", 193, $350+.
Vase, 10", 1353, $250-300.

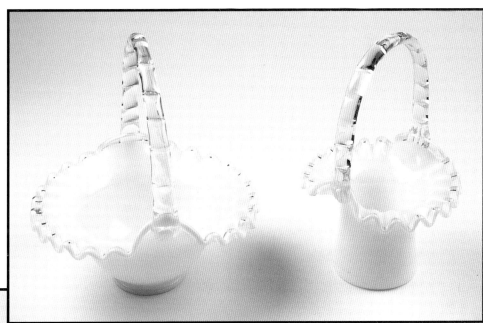

Basket, 7": 203, $125-150; Basket, 4": 1924, $100-125. *Courtesy of Alice and James Rose.*

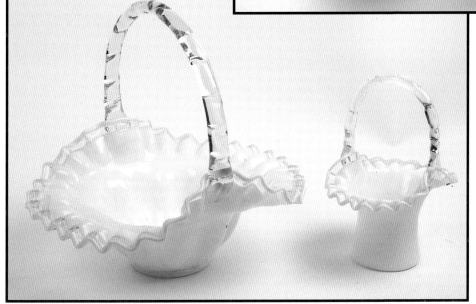

Basket, 10": 192, $200-225; Basket, 4": 1924, $100-125.

Back: Basket: 37, $350-400; Basket: 37, $350-400; Vase: 37, $200-225; Vase, Fan: 37, $200-225. *Courtesy of Alice and James Rose.*

Vase, Oval Crimp: 37, $200-225; Vase, Jack In Pulpit Crimp: 37, $200-225; Vase, Pie Crust Crimp: 37, $200-225.

Bonbon, 5", Tri-crimp: 36, $45-55; Bonbon, 5": 36, $45-55.

Bowl, 7", Pie Crust Crimp: 203, $55-65; Bowl, 7", D.C.: 203, $55-65.

Bowl, 10": 192, $125-150.

Bowl, 10", Tri-crimp: 1522, $90-110.

Bowl, 13", Special Rolled Edge: 1535, $200+.

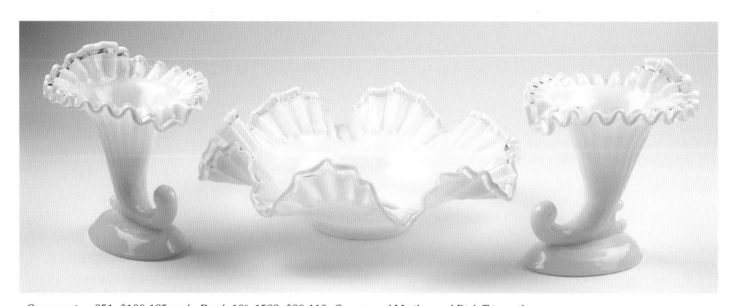

Cornucopias: 951, $100-125 each; Bowl, 10": 1522, $90-110. *Courtesy of Marilyn and Dick Trierweiler.*

Cornucopias: 951, $100-125 each; Epergne: 1522, $250-275. *Courtesy of Lynne and Gary Virden.*

Left:
Epergne: 1522,
$250-275.

Right:
Bottle, 7": 192,
$150-200. *Courtesy
of Norma and Melvin
Lampton.*

Flat Comport (Sweetmeat): 680, $125-150; Comport, Footed:
$75-85. *Courtesy of Lynne and Gary Virden.*

Candy, Covered, Footed: 206, $200+. This candy was
supposed to have been made with a clear ring on the upper
edge of the base of the candy. When the ring was applied, it
would pop off, so it was finally marketed without the ring on
the base. Add 50% more for bases with rings!

Top Hat: 1924, $100+. *Courtesy of Jan Hollingsworth.*

Jug, 6": 192, $125-150. *Courtesy of Norma and Melvin Lampton.*

Jug, Squat: 192, $250+.

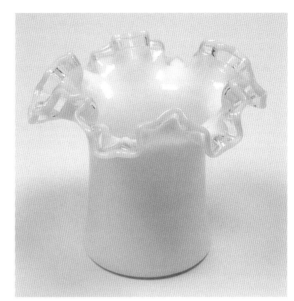

Vase, 5", Jack in the Pulpit Crimp: 1924, $45-55.

Vase, 4.5": 203, $45-55; Vase, 8": 186, $55-65; Vase, 5": 1924, $45-55.

Below:
Vase, 6": 36, $65-75; Vase, 4": 36, $45-55; Vase, 4", Tri-crimp: 36, $45-55; Vase, Fan, 6": 36, $75-85; Vase, Fan, 4": 36, $55-65.

Vase, Fan, 6": 36, $75-85; Vase, 6", Jack In the Pulpit Crimp: 36, $65-75; Vase, 6", D.C.: 36, $65-75; Vase, 6", Tri-crimp: 36, $65-75.

Vase, 6": 192, $45-55.

Vase, oval, 4.5": 203; Vase, 4.5", D.C.: 203. $55-65 each.

Vase, 5.5", Tri-crimp: 192, $45-55; Vase, 5.5": 192, $45-55; Vase, 5.5", JIP: 192, $45-55; Vase, 8": 192, $100-125. Vase, 5": 192, $75-85.

Silver Rose: 1956-1957/
Silver Turquoise: 1956-1959

Silver Rose and Silver Turquoise were introduced in 1956. Items that seldom appear are the footed square bowl in both colors, the 13" basket, either epergne, and the hurricane lamp in Silver Turquoise.

Item Description	Mould Number	Silver Rose	Silver Turquoise
Basket, 7"	7237	$70-85	$35-45
Basket, 13"	7233		$300-350
Bonbon, 5.5"	7225	$20-25	$15-20
Bowl, 7"	7227	$35-45	
Bowl, 10"	7224		$50-65
Bowl, 13"	7223		$75-90
Bowl, footed square	7330	$150-175	$85-100
Candlestick	7271		$30-40 each
Candlestick	7272		$45-55 each
Comport, footed	7228	$35-45	$25-35
Epergne, 1 horn, footed	7202		$125-150
Epergne, 1 horn, flat	7200		$150-175
Lamp, hurricane	7290		$175-200
Plate, 8.5"	7217		$35-45
Cake Plate	7213	$125-150	$100-125
Relish, Handled	7333	$50-65	$35-45

Basket, 7": 7237, YOP: 1956-57. *Author's Collection.*

Basket, 7": 7237, YOP: 1957-59; Basket, 13": 7233, YOP: 1956-58. *Courtesy of Alice and James G. Rose. See text for values.*

Bowl, 7": 7227; Bonbon, 5": 7225, YOP: ST: 195-59; SR: 1956-57.

Bowl, 10": 7224.

Bowl, Footed square 7330, YOP: ST: 1956-59; SR: 1956-57;
Candlesticks; 7271, YOP: 1956-59. *Courtesy of Jayne Lewis.*

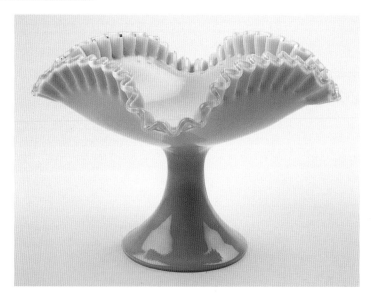

Bowl, Footed, Square: 7330,
YOP: ST: 1956-59; SR: 1956-57.

Bowl, Footed, Square: 7330. Top View.

Comport: 7228, YOP: ST: 1956-59; SR: 1956-57.

Relish, Handled: 7333, YOP: 195-57. Plate, 8.5": 7217, YOP: 1956; Relish, Handled: 7333, YOP: 1956-59.
Courtesy of Laurie and Rich Karman.

Epergne, Footed, 1 Horn: 7202, YOP: 1956-58; Candlestick: 7272, YOP: 1956-58; Not pictured: Epergne, Flat, 1 Horn: 7200, YOP: 1956-58. *Courtesy of Caryl Graham.*

Cake Plate, Footed: 7213, YOP: ST: 1956-59.

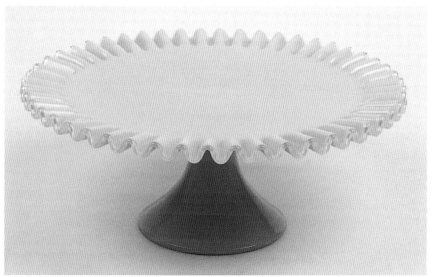

Lamp, Hurricane: 7290, YOP: 1/1956-6/56.
Courtesy of Eileen and Dale Robinson.

Cake Plate, Footed: 7213, YOP: SR: 1956-57.

Spanish Lace: MG: 1958-1964; RP: 1954-1957; BP/GP: 1954; Turquoise: 1955-1956

Made in Milk Glass and Pastel Milk Glass, Spanish Lace proved to be a popular line. Do not confuse this pattern with the Silver Crest Spanish Lace. These items do not have the crest on them. Made only in a Footed Cake Plate and a Footed Shallow Bowl, both items are rapidly disappearing off the market.

Shallow Bowl: 3513, YOP: 1955-58, RP: $55-65, MG: $35-45.

Cake Plate: 3513, $35-45 (pastel colors, $55-65)

Swirl: MG: 1954-1956;
Pastel Colors: 1954

Inspired by a Hobb's pattern of the same name, Swirl was first introduced in 1954 in Pastel Milk Glass, and White Milk Glass. Made in several interesting items, the pattern was not in Fenton's regular line for very long. Watch for the Cruet, Candleholders, and the Vanity Set, as these items seem to be the most scarce.

Not Pictured: Milk Glass

Salt/Pepper, 7001, YOP: 1954-56, $15-20.
Mayo, 7004, YOP: 1954-55, $20-25.

Vanity, Set, 7005, YOP: 1954-55, $100-125.
Sugar/Creamer, YOP: 7006, 1954, $15-20 each.
Bowl, 11", 7021, YOP: 1954-55, $25-30.
Bowl, Deep, 11", 7025, YOP: 1954, $25-30.
Candleholders, 7073, YOP: 1954-55, $20-25 each.

Not Pictured: Pastel Colors

Bowl, 11", 7021, $40-50.
Mayonnaise, 7004, $30-35.

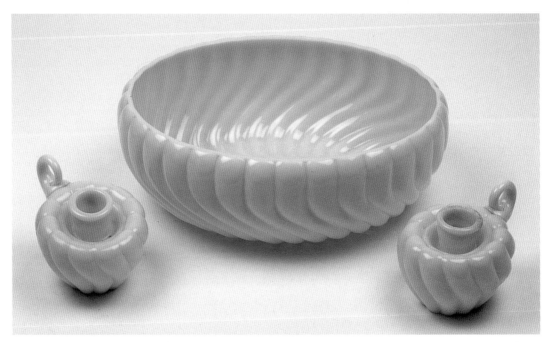

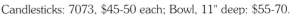

Candlesticks: 7073, $45-50 each; Bowl, 11" deep: $55-70.

Shakers: 7001, $35-45 pair; Cruet: 7063, $45-55. *Courtesy of Betty Merrell.*

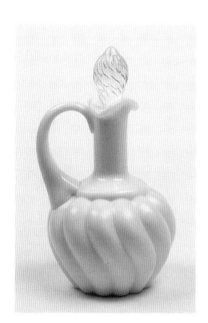

Cruet: 7063, YOP: 1954-55, $35-40. Courtesy *of Norma and Melvin Lampton.*

Cologne: 7005, $50-60; Powder Jar: $55-75; Vase: 7056, $25-35.

Creamer: 7006, $35-40; Sugar, Covered: 7006, $40-50.

Vase, 6": 7056, YOP: 1954-59, $15-20. *Courtesy of Diane and Tom Rohow.*

Teardrop: MG: 1958-1966;
Turquoise: 1955-1958

Teardrop is a pattern that was inspired by a condiment set produced by Dithridge & Co. in the 1880s. Teardrop was only produced in Turquoise in the Condiment Set and Flat Candy Dish; however, the pattern was made in a multitude of item in Milk Glass. It is a shame that none of the Milk Glass items have ever appeared in Turquoise! Sadly, Turquoise was about to be discontinued when Milk Glass Teardrop was introduced. Scarce items include the Cruet, Footed Candy, Footed Cake Plate, and Candleholders.

Condiment set, four piece, tray/handle, mustard, shakers: 6906, $140-150; Candy Box, Covered: 6985, $65-75. *Author's Collection.*

Sandwich Tray: 6997, YOP: 1957-58, $30-35; Bowl, 9": 6929, YOP: 1957-58, $35-40. *Courtesy of Bev and Jon Spencer.*

Candy: 6985, YOP: 1955-58, $30-35. *Courtesy of Betty and Ike Hardman.*

Cruet: 6963, YOP: 1957-58, $55-65.
Courtesy of Betty and Ike Hardman.

Creamer/Sugar: 6901, YOP: 1958, $20-25 each; Candy: 6985, YOP: 1955-58, $30-35; Candy Box, Footed: 6981, YOP: 1957, $55-65; Candleholders: 6974, YOP: 1957-58, $20-25. *Courtesy of Bev and Jon Spencer.*

Cake Plate, Footed: 6913, YOP: 1957-58, $55-75. *Courtesy of Bev and Jon Spencer.*

Condiment Set: 6909, YOP: 1955-62, $75-100. Items separately: Mustard: 6989, YOP: 1955-62, $15-20; Salt/Pepper: 6906, YOP: 1955-66, $20-25. *Courtesy of JR Antiques.*

Wave Crest: MG: 1957-1964

Inspired by a Wave Crest Box that Frank Fenton bought at an antique show in the early 1950s, Fenton developed Wave Crest into a complete pattern, including vases, jugs, a covered candy, and a pair of unique shakers. Wave Crest was made only in Milk Glass in the shakers, two sizes of jugs, and the candy. Any item in this pattern is considered very scarce.

Not Pictured: Wave Crest

Jug, 6", 6066, YOP: 7/1955-7/56, $15-20.

Salt/Pepper: 6006, YOP: 1957-64, $15-20; Jug, 6.5": 6068, YOP: 7/1955-7/56, $15-20. Not Pictured: Jug, 6": 6066, 7/1955-7/56, $15-20.

Candy: 6080, YOP: 1955-7/59, $35-45. *Courtesy of Diane Rohow.*

Wild Rose & Bowknot: MG: 1961-1962

Made from old McKee moulds, Wild Rose & Bowknot was produced in Milk Glass at the same time that it was produced in Overlay. One very scarce item to watch for is the squat pitcher, which was only made in Milk Glass.

Not Pictured: Wild Rose & Bowknot

Vase, 5", 2855, YOP: 1961, $15-20.
Vase, 7.5", 2857, YOP: 1961, $20-25.

Vase, 8": 2858, YOP: 1961, $35-45. *Courtesy of Norma and Melvin Lampton.*

Pitcher: 2865, YOP: 1961-7/62, $45-50.

Shakers: 2806, YOP: 1961, $15-20. *Courtesy of Bobbie & Harold Morgan.*

Vase from Lamp Shade, $45-55.; *Courtesy of Cindy and Rick Blais.*

Window Pane: MG: 1960-1961

A variation of Beatty's Honey Comb pattern, Window Pane is seldom seen in any item in Milk Glass.

Not Pictured: Window Pane

Basket, 6137, YOP: 1960, $35-40.
Candy Box, 6180, YOP: 1960, $25-30.
Medium Vase, 6158, YOP: 1960-61, $15-20.

Vase, 4": 6152, $10-15.

Old Virginia Glass: 1959-1970s

In 1960, Fenton first marketed their Old Virginia Glass (OVG), a line made for trading stamp companies, warehouse catalogs, and outlet stores. Fenton first introduced the Thumbprint line, in Milk Glass, and then followed with other patterns in other colors. In 1967, Desert Tree (Cactus) was issued through Old Virginia Glass, followed by Daisy and Button in Milk Glass in the late 1960s and Fine Cut and Block in the 1970s.

Beginning in the early 1970s, Fenton issued all its Old Virginia Glass items with the OVG logo, as the company had started to mark its own items with the Fenton logo.

Old Virginia Glass was discontinued in 1979, as most of its outlets became a thing of the past.

Fine Cut & Block: MG: 1970s

This pattern was developed for OVG in the 1970s as a companion line for Daisy & Button. Several interesting items were made, including the Candle Bowl and the Fairy Light.

Not Pictured: Fine Cut & Block

Covered Sugar/Creamer, 9103, $20-30 pair.
Fairy Light, 9102, $20-25.
Salt/Pepper, 9016, $15-20.
Compote, 9120, $15-20.
Vase, Swung, Medium, 9158, $20-25.
Candle Bowl, 9172, $20-25.

Candy Box: 9180, $30-35.

Basket, 7": 9137, $25-30; Vase, Large Swung: 9152, $30-35.

Thumbprint: MG: 1955-1962

Introduced in 1955 as a pattern to be sold exclusive through trading stamp catalogs and mail order houses, Thumbprint was, in reality, competition to Fenton's own Hobnail pattern, but with a small catch. In 1952, when Fenton Art Glass set up its present marketing plan, it promised its representatives that it would not offer the company's regular patterns to other sales people. As the Hobnail pattern was one of Fenton's regular lines, it would be impossible of make it accessible to outlets such as trading stamp catalogs and wholesale catalogs without breaking promises to its representatives. So Fenton developed the Thumbprint pattern for those ventures. Thumbprint became immensely successful. Fenton continued working in this vein for a number of years, selling Hobnail through its own company, and offering the Thumbprint pattern to wholesalers, until it developed it's Old Virginia Glass line. With the introduction of Old Virginia Glass, Fenton incorporated the Thumbprint pattern into that line. Several years after that, Fenton discontinued Thumbprint in Milk Glass, and recreated it in the Colonial Colors, which sold in its own line.

Not Pictured: Thumbprint

Goblet, 4445, $10-15.
Basket, 8.5", 4438, $25-30.
Handled Basket, 4437, $20-25.
Sugar/Creamer, 4403, $25-35 each.
Square Planter, 4497, $10-15.

Chip 'n' Dip: 4404, $45-55. *Courtesy of Sharen and Al Creery.*

Back: Bud Vase: 4456, $10-15; Oval Basket, 6.5": 4430, $25-35; Nut Dish: 4428, $15-20. Front: Low Candlesticks: 4474, $15-20 each.

Front: Low Candlesticks: 4474, $15-20 each. Back: Tall Candlesticks: 4473, $20-30 each. Center: Large Bowl: 4427, $45-55. *Courtesy of Williamstown Antique Mall.*

Tall Candlesticks: 4473, $20-30 each; Large Bowl: 4427, $45-55. *Courtesy of Sharen and Al Creery.*

Epergne: 4401, $90-100. *Courtesy of Bobbie & Harold Morgan.*

Hanging Planter: 4405, $65-75. *Courtesy of Sharen and Al Creery.*

Punch Set: 4406, $150-200. *Courtesy of Williamstown Antique Mall.*

Cake Plate: 4413, $40-50.

Low Candy: 4480, $25-35; Wedding Compote (Candy): 4484, $30-55; Oval Candy: 4486, $20-30. *Courtesy of Sharen and Al Creery.*

Shakers: 4408, $15-20.

Hurricane Lamp: 4498, $45-55. *Courtesy of Williamstown Antique Mall.*

Hurricane Lamp: 4498 Early Version, $55-65. *Courtesy of Williamstown Antique Mall.*

Lavabo: 4467, $90-100. *Courtesy of Sharen and Al Creery.*

Tidbit: 4494, $35-40. *Courtesy of Sharen and Al Creery.*

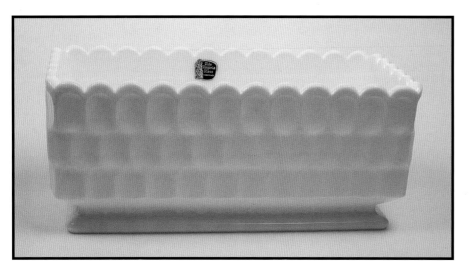

Planter: 4490, $25-30.

Glossary

Terms and phrases used in the glass making business.

Batch: A mixture of sand, soda ash, lime, and other chemicals that modify the color or characteristics of the glass. Once properly mixed, batch is then inserted into a pot furnace or day tank heated to 2,500 degrees Fahrenheit, thereby fusing the batch into the molted glass.

Blank: A blank is a piece of glass that has been formed, shaped, sent through the lehr, and is now ready to be processed by cutting, sand carving, or decorating – by the company producing the blank, by a glass decorating company, or by a glass cutting shop. In short, a blank is a piece that is ready to be processed further.

Blocker: The person who shapes the glass fresh from the furnace and blows the first bubble of air through a blow pipe into the glass.

Blower: The person who manipulates the glass into shape and plunges it into a mould. He then forces it throughout the mould by blowing into it.

Carrying-in Worker: The person who takes finished article to the Lehr for final cooling.

Carry Over Worker: The person who carries over pieces of glass, just pressed from a mould, to the glory hole for reheating, so the finisher may put a final crimp and shape into the glass.

D.C.: A term used for pieces that have a second, larger crimp, in addition to the original smaller, tight ruffle on the pieces. (It might be noted that the first crimp is usually made by a crimping mould while the second crimp is made by pulling the glass down by hand with a tool designed for that purpose.)

Day Tanks: Direct fire furnaces in which glass is exposed to direct flames. Day tanks melt glass in twelve hours cycles, allowing the glass to be melted by night and worked in the day time. The cycle could also be reversed if needed.

Finisher: The skilled worker who changes the shape of the piece after it has come from the mould into its final form, which may be flared, crimped, cupped, or changed into one of many different shapes.

Gather: The still unformed glob of molten glass, fresh from the furnaces or day tanks.

Gatherer: The worker who gathers glass from the day tank and takes it to the mould.

Glory Hole: A small furnace heated to a temperature to about 2,500 degrees Fahrenheit which is used to reheat the glass so it can be reshaped by the finisher.

Hand Swinging: The process of reheating a tumbler, bowl, or other item of glass to the point where it is so molted that it can be twirled on the end of the pipe like a baton so that the centrifugal force will stretch the piece out into what we call a "swung vase."

Handler: The worker who applies handles for baskets, jugs, etc.

Hot Metal Works: The area where furnaces are located in a glass factory.

Jobbers: Wholesalers who do not make the glass but who act as distributors for the glass company to the retail stores. The jobber may sell the regular Fenton. The jobber also might have glass made from his own moulds or may have special glass made by the glass company from its moulds, sometimes in different colors or shapes. Once the glassware has been obtained, jobbers then distribute these items to the retailers throughout their territories.

Lehr: A long annealing oven heated to about 1,000 degrees in which the glass is placed after it has been made in the Hot Metal Department. The glass is placed on a conveyor belt inside the oven. The stresses and strains that have been put into the glass during the process of heating and chilling are relieved by bring all the parts of the glass piece to the same temperature. Then the conveyor belt moves the glass to a cooler temperature and gradually cools it down to room temperature.

Mould Blown: Glass that is force blown into moulds, either by mouth or mechanical air pressure.

NIL (Not in Line): An item that was not sold in the regular line, of a certain treatment or color, nor was offered in any of Fenton's catalogs. Usually a Not In Line item was a Sample (experimental) piece, used to test the market. It may also have been an item that was produced by special order, either for an individual, or another company, or a jobber.

Opaline Glass: Partially opaque glass that is translucent. It looks opaque but will transmit light. It is glass that is about halfway between transparent glass and opaque glass.

Opaque Glass: Glass that allows a limited amount of light to pass through it, showing little fire or translucence when held to the light.

Overlay Glass: Cased glass in which one layer is gathered over another.

Pressed Blown: Glass pressed into the mould and then forced to fill out the mould by blowing into it, either by mouth or mechanical air pressure.

Presser: The skilled glassworker who controls the temperature of the mould, cuts off the glass when it is dropped by the gathers, controls the weight of the glass that goes into the mould, and pulls the lever of the press which brings down the plunger to force the glass into each part of the press mould. He also removes the plunger and opens the mould to remove the glass.

Ringer: The worker who spins a thin ring of different colored molten glass to the edge of the piece, thereby forming the glass we call Crest glass.

Spot mould: Sometimes called an optic mould, this mould is used to create a pattern within the glass. The mould itself has a pattern that is transferred to the glass. After reheating, the glass is then blown into a second plain mound with no pattern. When the piece is made from opalescent (or any other heat sensitive glass), chilling and reheating the patterns creates opaque areas, while other parts remain clear.

Turn: Four hours of production will constitute a "turn's work." The number of pieces made in that four-hour period depends on the size, complexity, and shape of the piece.

Warming-In Worker: The person who reheats the glass in the glory hole, removes it, and takes it to the finisher for further shaping.

Bibliography

Books

Fenton Art Glass Collectors of America. *Caught in the Butterfly Net*. Williamstown, WV: Fenton Art Glass Club of America, Inc., 1991.

_____. *Fenton Catalog Pages*. Reprint. Williamstown, WV: Fenton Art Glass Club of America, Inc., 1986.

Florence, Gene. *Collectible Glassware from the '40s, '50s, '60s*. 3d ed. Paducah, KY: Schroeder, 1996.

Griffith, Shirley. *Pictorial Review of Fenton's White Hobnail Milk Glass*. N. p., 1994.

Heacock, William. *Fenton Glass: The 2nd Twenty Five Years*. Marietta, OH: O-Val Advertising Corp., 1980.

_____. *Fenton Glass: The 3rd Twenty Five Years*. Marietta, OH: O-Val Advertising Corp., 1989.

_____. *Victorian Colored Pattern Glass Book II: Opalescent Glass A to Z*. Marietta, OH: Antique Publications, 1975.

_____. *Victorian Colored Pattern Glass Book III: Syrups, Sugar Shakers A to Z*. Marietta, OH: Antique Publications, 1976.

Heacock, William and William Gamble. *Victorian Colored Pattern Glass Book IX: Cranberry Opalescent Glass A to Z*. Marietta, OH: Antique Publications, 1987.

Lafferty, James Sr. *The Forties Revisited*. James Lafferty Sr., 1968.

Lecher, Mildred and Ralph. *The World of Salt Shakers*. Paducah, KY: Schroeder, 1992.

Measell, James, ed. *Fenton Glass: The '80s Decade*. Marietta, OH: Antique Publications, 1996.

_____. *Fenton Glass: The '90s Decade*. Marietta, OH: Antique Publications, 2000.

Walk, John. *Fenton Glass Compendium, 1940-70*. Atglen, PA: Schiffer Publishing, 1991.

_____. *Fenton Glass Compendium, 1970-85*. Atglen, PA: Schiffer Publishing, 1991.

_____. *Fenton Rarities, 1940-1985*. Atglen, PA: Schiffer Publishing, 2002.

Walk, John and Joseph Gates. *The Big Book of Fenton Glass, 1940-70*. 2d ed. Atglen, PA: Schiffer Publishing, 1998.

Whitmyer, Kenn & Margaret. *Bedroom and Bathroom Glassware of the Depression Years*. Paducah, KY: Schroeder, 1990.

_____. *Fenton Art Glass Patterns*. Paducah, KY: Schroeder, 1939-80.

Periodicals

Depression Glass Daze, 1980-1997.
Glass Collector's Digest, 1986-1997.
Glass Review, 1978-1987.